The Ultimate Ninja Dual Zone
Air Fryer Cookbook
with Pictures

1600 Days Easy & Amazing Recipes for Beginners to Make Your Meals Taste Fabulous| Master the Art of the Dual Zone Air Fryer

Alan N. Collins

Copyright© 2023 By Alan N. Collins
All Rights Reserved

This book is copyright protected. It is only for personal use.
You cannot amend, distribute, sell, use,
quote or paraphrase any part of the content within this book,
without the consent of the author or publisher.
Under no circumstances will any blame or
legal responsibility be held against the publisher,
or author, for any damages, reparation,
or monetary loss due to the information contained within this book,
either directly or indirectly.

Disclaimer Notice:

Please note the information contained within this
document is for educational and entertainment purposes only.
All effort has been executed to present accurate,
up to date, reliable, complete information.
No warranties of any kind are declared or implied.
Readers acknowledge that the author is not engaged
in the rendering of legal,
financial, medical or professional advice.
The content within this book has been derived from various sources.
Please consult a licensed professional before attempting any
techniques outlined in this book.
By reading this document,
the reader agrees that under no circumstances is the
author responsible for any losses,
direct or indirect,
that are incurred as a result of the use of the
information contained within this document, including,
but not limited to, errors, omissions, or inaccuracies.

Contents

Introduction 1
Chapter I: Unleashing the Power of Air Frying 1
Chapter II: Getting to Know the Ninja Air Fryer 1
Why Choose the Ninja Dual Zone? 2
How to Use the Ninja Air Fryer 3
Tips and Tricks for Using the Ninja Air Fryer 4
Cleaning and Maintenance 5

Chapter 1 Breakfast 6
Biscuit Donuts 7
Eccles Cakes 7
Spinach and Feta Muffins 8
Buttermilk Pancakes 8
Lobster Omelette 9
Butteries 9
Shropshire Fidget Pie 10
Eggs in Purgatory 10
Staffordshire Oatcakes 11
Crispy Bacon and Tomato Sandwich 11
Bacon and Cheese Scones 12
Irish Soda Bread 12

Chapter 2 Lunch 13
Fried Pickles 14
Melton Mowbray Pork Pie 14
Bubble and Squeak Scotch Egg Soldiers 15
Cornish Pasty Potato Bites 15
Chicken Liver Pâté Stuffed Mushrooms 16
Pickled Egg and Bacon Toasted Sandwiches 16
Bangers and Mash Croquettes 17

Currywurst Spring Rolls 17

Chapter 3 Dinner.. 18
Stilton and Broccoli Quiche 19
Scampi and Chips 19
Lamb Kofta Kebabs 20
Pheasant with Cranberry Sauce 20
Chicken Fajitas and chips 21
Mexican Chicken and Sweet Potatoes 21
Nando's Loaded Chicken Chips 22
Tikka Chicken Salad with Popadoms 22
Peri Peri Chicken Wraps and Chips 23
Garlic Parmesan Carrot Fries 23
Honey Mustard Glazed Pork Tenderloin 24
Lemon Herb Roast Chicken 24
Pesto Chicken Pasta 25
Baked Cod with Herbed Breadcrumbs 25
Salmon en Papillote 26
Chicken Parmesan 26
Stuffed Bell Peppers 27
Teriyaki Salmon 27

Chapter 4 Beef, Pork and Lamb 28
Beef and Ale Baked Beans 29
Pork and Black Pudding Roulade 29
Lamb and Apricot Tagine 30
Filipino Fried Pork (Pritong Baboy) 30
Cajun Pork Fillet with Sweet Potatoes 31
Tikka Pork Chops 31
Beef and Tattie Scones 32
Pork and Chorizo Cassoulet 32
Lamb and Roasted Pepper Quiche 33
Lamb and caramelised Onion Gravy 33
Lamb and Tomato Tarts 34

Beef and Horseradish Suet Pudding 34

Chapter 5 Fish and Seafood 35
Bass with Sauce Vierge 36
Monkfish with Parma Ham 36
Lobster and Scallop Thermidor 37
Monkfish Cheeks 37
Mussels in Cider 38
Sea Bass with Fennel and Blood Orange 38
Hake and Chorizo Stew 39
Grilled Sardines 39
Plaice Goujons 40
Tuna Nicoise Salad 40
Skate with Black Butter 41
Seafood Paella... 41
Baked Gurnard with Cherry Tomato 42

Chapter 6 Sides and Appetisers 43
Courgette Fries 44
Baked Camembert with RedCurrant Jelly 44
Parmesan and Garlic Roasted Brussels Sprouts 45
Liver and Bacon on Crusty Bread 45
Scotch Woodcock (Anchovy on Toast) 46
Crispy Baked Goat Cheese Balls 46
Bubble and Squeak Patties 47
Bacon-Wrapped Dates with Blue Cheese 47
Smoked Haddock Scotch Eggs with Hollandaise Sauce 48
Black Pudding Crostini with Pear Chutney 48
Ploughman's Platter Bites 49
Stilton and Pear Crostini 49
Marmite and Cheese Swirls 50

Chapter 7 Vegan and Veggies 51
Vegan Falafel 52

Roasted Vegetable Kebabs … 52
Baked Sweet Potato Fries … 53
Vegan Sausages … 53
Stuffed Mushrooms … 54
Roasted Brussels Sprouts … 54
Baked Butternut Squash Risotto … 55
Fried Tofu Stir-fry … 55
Vegan Spring Rolls … 56
Roasted Cauliflower Steaks … 56
Baked Aubergine Parmesan … 57
Fried Plantain Slices … 57
Vegan Chickpea Patties … 58
Vegan Potato Rosti … 58
Roasted Tomato and Chickpea Salad … 59

Chapter 8 Sweet Snacks and Desserts … 60

Chocolate and Beetroot Cake … 61
Raspberry Meringue Roulade … 61
Cherry and Almond Frangipane … 62
Rhubarb and Ginger Crumble … 62
Sticky Ginger Parkin … 63
Orange Marmalade Bread Pudding … 63
Coffee and Walnut Swiss Roll … 64
Sticky Fig Parkin … 64

Introduction

Welcome to the flavorful world of air frying! I am thrilled to invite you on an exciting culinary journey as we explore the Ninja Air Fryer Cookbook . I want to connect with you on a personal level, sharing my experiences and passion for cooking, so together we can unlock the full potential of this amazing kitchen appliance.

Chapter I: Unleashing the Power of Air Frying

In this chapter, we will delve into the basics of air frying, empowering you with the knowledge to create tantalizing dishes with ease.

Air frying is a cooking method that uses circulating hot to evenly cook food, it a crispy texture without the need for excess oil. It has become increasingly popular as a healthier alternative to deep frying.

To get started with air frying, you will need an air fryer. These appliances come in various sizes and styles, so choose one that suits your needs. Most air fryers have a temperature control mechanism and a timer, allowing you to customize the cooking settings for different recipes.

Here are some key tips to keep in mind when using an air fryer£º

1. Preheat the air fryer: Just like with traditional ovens, it's important to preheat your air fryer before cooking. This helps to ensure even cooking and better results.

2. Use the right amount of oil: While air frying requires less oil than deep frying, some recipes may still call for a small amount of oil. Be sure to follow the recipe guidelines or use an oil spray to lightly coat the food.

3. Arrange the food evenly: To achieve even cooking, arrange the food in a single layer in the air fryer basket, making sure not to overcrowd it. This allows the hot air to circulate freely around the food.

4. Shake or flip the food: During cooking, shake the basket or flip the food halfway through to ensure all sides are evenly cooked. This will help to achieve a crispy exterior and tender interior.

5. Adjust cooking time and temperature: Different foods require different cooking times and temperatures. Refer to recipe guidelines or experiment by starting with lower cooking times or temperatures, then adjusting as needed.

Chapter II: Getting to Know the Ninja Air Fryer

Join me as we explore the incredible lineup of Ninja Air Fryers, highlighting their unique features and benefits. From the top-selling favorites to the latest innovations, we'll uncover the perfect Ninja Air Fryer for your cooking adventures.

Absolutely! Let's dive into the world of Ninja Air Fryers and discover their incredible lineup of features and benefits.

1. Ninja Foodi Deluxe XL Air Fryer:
The Ninja Foodi Deluxe XL Air Fryer offers a spacious cooking capacity, allowing you to cook for large gatherings or families. With its innovative TenderCrisp Technology, you can air fry, roast, bake, broil, and dehydrate your favorite meals. It also comes with a reversible rack that increases cooking versatility.

2. Ninja Foodi 5-in-1 Indoor Grill with 4-Quart Air Fryer:
If you crave the taste of grilled food, then the Ninja Foodi 5-in-1 Indoor Grill with 4-Quart Air Fryer is perfect for you. This versatile appliance allows you to grill, air fry, bake, roast, and dehydrate food all in one. It comes with a Smart Cook System that ensures even cooking throughout your ingredients.

3. Ninja Foodi 8-in-1 Digital Air Fry Oven:
The Ninja Foodi 8-in-1 Digital Air Fry Oven combines the functions of an air fryer and a toasteroven. It has a spacious cooking capacity that enables you to cook multiple dishes at once. The oven includes eight cooking functions, including air frying, baking, toasting, roasting, and more. It also comes with a digital display for easy temperature and time adjustments.

4. Ninja Air Fryer Max XL:
The Ninja Air Fryer Max XL is perfect for those who want a compact yet high-capacity air fryer. With a 5.5-quart cooking basket, you can cook larger portions for the whole family. It operates with minimal oil, making it a healthier alternative to traditional frying. The air fryer also features a wide temperature range and a digital control panel for precise cooking.

5. Ninja Foodi Dual Zone Air Fryer:
If you're looking for ultimate versatility, the Ninja Foodi Dual Zone Air Fryer is a great choice. It comes with two independent cooking zones, allowing you to cook two different foods simultaneously at different temperatures and times. This feature comes in handy during meal preparation and saves you time in the kitchen.

These are just a few examples of the incredible lineup of Ninja Air Fryers available. They offer a wide range of functions, sizes, and features to cater to different cooking needs. Happy exploring and finding the perfect Ninja Air Fryer for your cooking adventures.

Why Choose the Ninja Dual Zone?

The Ninja Air Fryer is an excellent appliance, one I'd recommend you add to your Kitchen. It can definitely save you a lot of stress and make your cooking faster, better and healthier. Here are some reasons to choose the Ninja Dual Zone Air Fryer:

- Powerful Convection: The Ninja Dual Zone Air Fryer boasts true surround convection technology, providing up to 10 times the convection power compared to traditional full-size convection ovens. This means faster, crispier, and juicier results.
- Versatile Cooking: With up to 10 cooking

modes in one appliance, you can air fry, roast, bake, whole roast, broil, toast, make bagels, dehydrate, reheat, and even cook pizza. It's a kitchen workhorse that can handle various cooking tasks.
- Precision Cooking: The integrated Foodi Smart Thermometer ensures perfect doneness at the touch of a button, eliminating guesswork and helping you achieve your desired level of cooking from rare to well done.
- Time-Saving: Dual zone air fryers offer quick family meals with a 90-second oven preheat time. It is up to 30% faster cooking than traditional full-size convection ovens. This is especially useful for busy households.
- Extra-Large Capacity: The appliance provides 2-level cooking without the need for rotation. It can accommodate large meals, such as a 5-lb chicken with a sheet pan of vegetables, two 12-inch pizzas, or even a 12-lb turkey. Perfect for larger gatherings or meal prepping.
- Healthier Cooking: Enjoy healthier meals with the Air Fry function, which can reduce fat by up to 75% compared to traditional deep frying, tested against hand-cut, deep-fried French fries. Plus, it delivers up to 30% crispier results compared to a standard convection oven.
- User-Friendly: The digital display handle makes it easy to select functions, and the

oven rack positions illuminate based on your choice. The settings remain secure when the door is open, preventing accidental changes.
- Effortless for Entertaining: You can prepare two sheet pan meals simultaneously. It's perfect for hosting gatherings or simplifying your weekly meal preparation.

How to Use the Ninja Air Fryer

Using a Ninja Air Fryer is relatively straightforward. Here's a basic guide:
- Read the Manual: Start by reading the user manual that comes with your Ninja Air Fryer. This will provide specific instructions and safety guidelines for your particular model.
- Preparation: Place the air fryer on a clean, flat, and heat-resistant surface. Ensure there's enough space around the air fryer for proper ventilation.
- Preheat the Air Fryer (if required): Some recipes may recommend preheating the air fryer. If so, set the desired temperature and let it preheat for a few minutes.
- Prepare Your Ingredients: Season or marinate your food as desired. Place your ingredients in a suitable container or air fryer basket/tray. Ensure they are in a single layer for even cooking.
- Select the Function: Choose the cooking function that best suits your dish. Ninja Air Fryers typically offer a variety of functions like Air Fry, Roast, Bake, etc. Use

the control panel to select the appropriate function.
- Set the Time and Temperature: Use the control panel to set the cooking time and temperature. Refer to your recipe or the air fryer's guidelines for the recommended settings.
- Start Cooking: Press the start button to begin the cooking process.
- Check and Shake (if needed): Depending on your recipe, you may need to pause the cooking process to shake or flip your food for even results. Some air fryers even have a reminder to do this.
- Monitor Progress: Keep an eye on your food as it cooks. You can usually observe the cooking progress through the air fryer's transparent door or lid.
- Finish and Serve: When the cooking time is complete, carefully open the air fryer. Be cautious, as it will be hot. Use oven mitts or a towel to remove the food and place it on a serving plate.
- Let it Cool: Allow the air fryer to cool down before cleaning it.
- Cleaning: After each use, clean the air fryer's removable parts like the basket, tray, and crumb tray. Many parts are dishwasher-safe for convenience. Read on for tips on how to clean your Ninja Air Fryer.
- Storage: Once cleaned and completely cooled, store the air fryer in a safe and dry location.

Remember to refer to your specific Ninja Air Fryer's manual for model-specific instructions and safety precautions. Furthermore, always follow the recommended cooking times and temperatures for your recipes to ensure the best results.

Tips and Tricks for Using the Ninja Air Fryer

Based on my experience with Ninja Air Fryer, I'd like to share some pro tips and tricks with you to give you a head start with the Ninja Air Fryer. They include:
- Use the Match Cook feature to cook different foods at different temperatures. This is an excellent feature for cooking a meal for everyone in your family, especially if they have different dietary restrictions.
- Use the Smart Finish feature to finish cooking two different foods at the same time. You can cook the main course and side dish together.
- If you're cooking multiple batches of food, preheat the air fryer between batches. This will help to ensure that all of your food cooks evenly.
- Don't overcrowd the air fryer baskets. Overcrowding might prevent the hot air from circulating freely and can result in uneven cooking.
- Shake or toss the food halfway through cooking. This will help to ensure that the food cooks evenly.
- Use a little bit of oil on your food. Slight

oiling might be necessary to prevent the food from sticking to the air fryer baskets.
- Be careful when removing the food from the air fryer baskets. The baskets will be hot.
- Clean the air fryer baskets after each use. This will help to prevent the build-up of food and grease.
- Use parchment paper or a silicone baking mat in the air fryer baskets. This will help to prevent food from sticking and make cleanup easier.
- If you're cooking breaded foods, spray the breading with a little bit of oil before air frying for breading crispy.
- If you're cooking frozen foods, there is no need to thaw them before air frying. Simply place the frozen food in the air fryer basket and cook according to the package directions.
- To make your own air fryer croutons, cut bread into cubes and toss with some olive oil and seasonings. Air fry at 350 degrees Fahrenheit for 5-7 minutes or until the croutons are golden brown and crispy.
- To make your own air fryer popcorn, place a single layer of popcorn kernels in the air fryer basket. Air fry at 400 degrees Fahrenheit for 2-3 minutes, or until the popcorn is popped.

With a bit of practice, you'll be air-frying like a pro in no time!

Cleaning and Maintenance

Cleaning your Air Fryer is very important to ensure efficiency and longevity. I'd like to share my cleaning tips with you below:
- Unplug the air fryer and let it cool completely.
- Remove the air fryer basket and crisper tray. You can wash these parts by hand or in the dishwasher.
- Wipe the inside and outside of the air fryer with a damp cloth. Be careful not to get water into the electrical components of the air fryer.
- If there is any stubborn grease or food

residue, you can use a mild dish soap and water solution to clean it. Be sure to rinse the air fryer thoroughly with clean water after cleaning.
- Dry the air fryer completely before using it again.
- Clean the air fryer basket and crisper tray after each use. This will help to prevent the build-up of food and grease.
- If you're not using the air fryer basket or crisper tray, you can soak them in warm, soapy water for a few minutes before cleaning. This will help to loosen any stuck-on food.
- You can use a mild dish soap and water solution to clean the inside and outside of the air fryer. Be sure to rinse the air fryer thoroughly with clean water after cleaning.
- If there is any stubborn grease or food residue on the inside of the air fryer, you can use a baking soda paste to clean it.
- Make a paste with baking soda and water and apply it to the affected area. Let the paste sit for a few minutes before scrubbing it off with a damp cloth.
- To clean the heating element, use a soft brush to remove any food particles or grease. Be careful not to use any abrasive cleaners or scrubbers, as this could damage the heating element.
- With a bit of care and attention, your Ninja Air Fryer will stay clean and in good condition for many years to come.

Chapter 1
Breakfast

Biscuit Donuts

Prep time: 15 minutes Cook time: 10 minutes Serves 4

Ingredients
- 1 can refrigerated biscuit dough
- 2 tablespoons melted butter
- 60g granulated sugar
- 1 teaspoon ground cinnamon
- Optional: Icing or chocolate sauce for drizzling

Instructions
1. Preheat the Ninja Dual Zone Air Fryer to 350°F using the Air Fry mode.
2. Open the can of biscuit dough and separate the individual biscuits.
3. Cut a hole in the center of each biscuit to form the donut shape.
4. Brush both sides of the biscuits with melted butter.
5. In a shallow bowl, mix together 60g sugar and 1 teaspoon ground cinnamon.
6. Dip each biscuit in the cinnamon-sugar mixture, ensuring both sides are coated.
7. Place the biscuits in the air fryer basket, making sure they don't touch.
8. Air fry for about 8-10 minutes until the donuts are golden brown, turning them halfway through.
9. Once done, let them cool for a few minutes. Optionally, drizzle icing or chocolate sauce over the donuts.
10. Serve and enjoy your delicious Biscuit Donuts for a hearty breakfast.

Eccles Cakes

Prep time: 20 minutes Cook time: 15 minutes Serves 8

Ingredients
- 1 pack of puff pastry (store-bought or homemade)
- 150g currants or raisins
- 50g unsalted butter, softened
- 50g brown sugar
- 1 teaspoon ground cinnamon
- Milk for brushing
- Demerara sugar for sprinkling

Instructions
1. Preheat the Ninja Dual Zone Air Fryer to 375°F using the Bake mode.
2. Roll out the puff pastry on a floured surface.
3. In a bowl, mix together currants or raisins, softened butter, brown sugar, and ground cinnamon.
4. Spoon small portions of the fruit mixture onto the rolled-out pastry.
5. Fold the pastry over to encase the filling and seal the edges.
6. Cut into individual Eccles Cakes and place them on the air fryer basket.
7. Brush the tops with milk and sprinkle with demerara sugar.
8. Bake for about 15 minutes, or until the Eccles Cakes are golden brown.
9. Allow them to cool slightly before serving these delightful, sweet pastries.

Spinach and Feta Muffins

Prep time: 15 minutes   Cook time: 20 minutes   Serves 12

Ingredients
- 200g fresh spinach, chopped
- 100g feta cheese, crumbled
- 1 small onion, finely chopped
- 2 cloves garlic, minced
- 200g all-purpose flour
- 2 teaspoons baking powder
- 1/2 teaspoon baking soda
- 1/2 teaspoon salt   • 2 large eggs
- 150ml milk   • 80ml olive oil
- Freshly ground black pepper to taste

Instructions
1. Preheat the Ninja Dual Zone Air Fryer to 375°F using the Bake mode.
2. In a skillet, sauté chopped spinach, finely chopped onion, and minced garlic until the spinach wilts and the onion is translucent. Allow it to cool.
3. In a large bowl, whisk together all-purpose flour, baking powder, baking soda, and salt.
4. In a separate bowl, beat eggs and add milk and olive oil. Mix well.
5. Pour the wet ingredients into the dry ingredients and stir until just combined.
6. Fold in the sautéed spinach, crumbled feta, and freshly ground black pepper.
7. Line muffin cups with paper liners or grease them.
8. Spoon the batter into the muffin cups, filling each about two-thirds full.
9. Place the muffin cups in the air fryer basket.
10. Bake for about 18-20 minutes, or until a toothpick inserted into the centre comes out clean.
11. Allow to cool slightly before serving.

Buttermilk Pancakes

Prep time: 10 minutes   Cook time: 15 minutes   Serves 4

Ingredients
- 200g all-purpose flour
- 1 tablespoon sugar
- 1 teaspoon baking powder
- 1/2 teaspoon baking soda
- 1/4 teaspoon salt
- 240ml buttermilk
- 1 large egg
- 28g melted butter
- Additional butter for cooking
- Honey (optional)

Instructions
1. Preheat the Ninja Dual Zone Air Fryer to 375°F using the Bake mode.
2. In a bowl, whisk together 200g flour, 1 tablespoon sugar, baking powder, baking soda, and salt.
3. In another bowl, whisk together 240ml buttermilk, egg, and melted butter.
4. Pour the wet ingredients into the dry ingredients, stirring until just combined.
5. Grease the air fryer basket with a small amount of butter.
6. Pour 1/4 cup of batter onto the air fryer basket for each pancake.
7. Bake for about 12-15 minutes, or until the pancakes are golden brown.
8. Best served warm with honey if desired.

Lobster Omelette

| Prep time: 15 minutes | Cook time: 10 minutes | Serves 4 |

Ingredients
- 8 large eggs
- 200g cooked lobster meat, chopped
- Salt and pepper to taste
- 2 tablespoons chopped fresh chives
- 2 tablespoons olive oil

Instructions
1. Preheat the Ninja Dual Zone Air Fryer to 375°F using the Air Fry mode.
2. In a bowl, whisk together 8 eggs. Season with salt and pepper.
3. Add the chopped lobster meat and fresh chives to the eggs, stirring to combine.
4. Grease the air fryer basket with olive oil.
5. Pour the egg mixture into the basket.
6. Air fry for about 10 minutes, or until the omelette is set.
7. Once done, carefully remove the omelette from the air fryer basket.
8. Fold the omelette in half and transfer it to a serving plate.
9. Garnish with additional chopped chives if desired then serve hot.

Butteries

| Prep time: 20 minutes | Cook time: 15 minutes | Serves 4 |

Ingredients
- 300g all-purpose flour
- 1 teaspoon salt
- 200g unsalted butter, cold and cubed
- 150ml water, cold

Instructions
1. Preheat the Ninja Dual Zone Air Fryer to 400°F using the Bake mode.
2. In a large bowl, mix 300g flour and 1 teaspoon salt.
3. Add cold, cubed unsalted butter to the flour mixture. Use a pastry cutter or your fingers to rub the butter into the flour until it resembles coarse breadcrumbs.
4. Gradually add cold water, mixing until the dough comes together.
5. Roll out the dough on a floured surface to about 1/2 inch thickness.
6. Fold the dough into thirds, then roll it out again. Repeat this process two more times.
7. Cut the dough into squares or rounds.
8. Place the butteries on the air fryer basket, ensuring they are not touching.
9. Bake for about 15 minutes, or until the butteries are golden brown and flaky.
10. Serve the Butteries warm and enjoy the rich, flaky goodness.

Shropshire Fidget Pie

Prep time: 15 minutes   Cook time: 10 minutes   Serves 4

Ingredients
- 4 English muffins, split and toasted
- 4 slices smoked salmon
- 4 poached eggs
- Hollandaise sauce (store-bought or homemade)
- Chopped fresh chives for garnish

Instructions
1. Preheat the Ninja Dual Zone Air Fryer to 375°F using the Air Fry mode.
2. Toast the English muffins in the air fryer basket for about 3-5 minutes, or until they are golden brown.
3. Place a slice of smoked salmon on each toasted English muffin half.
4. Carefully poach the eggs using the air fryer.
5. Top each smoked salmon layer with a poached egg.
6. Drizzle hollandaise sauce over each poached egg.
7. Garnish with chopped fresh chives.
8. Serve immediately for the best flavour and taste.

Eggs in Purgatory

Prep time: 15 minutes   Cook time: 15 minutes   Serves 4

Ingredients
- 2 tablespoons olive oil
- 1 onion, finely chopped
- 2 cloves garlic, minced
- 1 teaspoon red pepper flakes (adjust to taste)
- 800g canned crushed tomatoes
- Salt and pepper to taste
- 4 eggs
- Fresh basil, chopped, for garnish

Instructions
1. Preheat the Ninja Dual Zone Air Fryer to 375°F using the Bake mode.
2. In a skillet or oven-safe dish, heat olive oil over medium heat.
3. Add finely chopped onion and sauté until translucent.
4. Stir in minced garlic and red pepper flakes, cooking for an additional minute.
5. Pour in the canned crushed tomatoes and season with salt and pepper. Simmer for about 10 minutes, allowing the flavours to meld.
6. Make small wells in the tomato mixture and carefully crack an egg into each well.
7. Transfer the skillet or dish to the air fryer basket.
8. Bake for approximately 15 minutes, or until the eggs are set to your liking.
9. Garnish with chopped fresh basil.
10. Serve hot, and enjoy this spicy and flavourful breakfast dish.

Staffordshire Oatcakes

Prep time: 10 minutes   Cook time: 15 minutes   Serves 4

Ingredients
- 200g oat flour
- 1 teaspoon baking powder
- 1/2 teaspoon salt
- 300ml milk
- 1 large egg
- Butter for greasing

Instructions
1. Preheat the Ninja Dual Zone Air Fryer to 375°F using the Bake mode.
2. In a bowl, whisk together 200g oat flour, baking powder, and salt.
3. In a separate bowl, mix together milk and a large egg.
4. Gradually add the wet ingredients to the dry ingredients, stirring until well combined.
5. Grease the air fryer basket with butter.
6. Pour a ladle of batter into the basket, spreading it evenly to form oatcakes.
7. Bake for about 12-15 minutes, or until the oatcakes are golden brown.
8. Repeat with the remaining batter.
9. Serve warm, and enjoy this unique and wholesome breakfast!

Crispy Bacon and Tomato Sandwich

Prep time: 10 minutes   Cook time: 15 minutes   Serves 2

Ingredients
- 4 slices of bread
- 8 slices crispy bacon
- 2 large tomatoes, thinly sliced
- Lettuce leaves
- Mayonnaise or preferred sauce

Instructions
1. Preheat the Ninja Dual Zone Air Fryer to 375°F using the Air Fry mode.
2. Lay out the bread slices.
3. On two slices, arrange crispy bacon, thinly sliced tomatoes, and lettuce leaves.
4. Spread mayonnaise or your preferred sauce on the other two slices of bread.
5. Place the mayo-spread slices on top of the bacon and tomato slices to form sandwiches.
6. Transfer the sandwiches to the air fryer basket.
7. Air fry for about 5 minutes, or until the sandwiches are golden brown and heated through.
8. Serve hot for a wholesome breakfast experience.

Bacon and Cheese Scones

Prep time: 15 minutes | Cook time: 12 minutes | Serves 6

Ingredients
- 250g all-purpose flour
- 1 tablespoon baking powder
- 1/2 teaspoon salt
- 100g cold unsalted butter, diced
- 100g crispy bacon, crumbled
- 100g grated cheddar cheese
- 150ml milk

Instructions
1. Preheat the Ninja Dual Zone Air Fryer to 375°F using the Bake mode.
2. In a large bowl, whisk together 250g flour, baking powder, and salt.
3. Add diced cold butter and rub it into the flour until the mixture resembles breadcrumbs.
4. Stir in crumbled crispy bacon and grated cheddar cheese.
5. Pour in milk and mix until just combined.
6. Turn the dough out onto a floured surface and gently knead.
7. Pat the dough into a round shape, about 1-inch thick.
8. Cut out scones using a round cutter and place them on the air fryer basket.
9. Bake for about 12 minutes, or until the scones are golden brown.
10. Serve the Bacon and Cheese Scones warm, and enjoy the savory goodness.

Irish Soda Bread

Prep time: 10 minutes | Cook time: 35 minutes | Serves 8

Ingredients
- 500g all-purpose flour
- 1 teaspoon baking soda
- 1 teaspoon salt
- 400ml buttermilk

Instructions
1. Preheat the Ninja Dual Zone Air Fryer to 400°F using the Bake mode.
2. In a large bowl, whisk together 500g flour, baking soda, and salt.
3. Make a well in the center and pour in the buttermilk.
4. Mix quickly until the dough comes together.
5. Turn the dough out onto a floured surface and gently shape it into a round loaf.
6. Place the loaf on the air fryer basket.
7. Bake for about 35 minutes, or until the bread is golden brown and sounds hollow when tapped.
8. Allow to cool slightly before slicing and serving.

Chapter 2
Lunch

Fried Pickles

Prep time: 15 minutes Cook time: 10 minutes Serves 4

Ingredients
- 1 jar pickles (about 400g), sliced
- 125g all-purpose flour
- 2 large eggs, beaten
- 120g breadcrumbs
- 1 teaspoon paprika
- 1/2 teaspoon garlic powder
- Salt and pepper to taste
- Cooking spray

Instructions
1. Preheat the Ninja Dual Zone Air Fryer to 375°F using the Air Fry mode.
2. Pat the pickle slices dry with a paper towel.
3. In one bowl, place the flour. In another, beat the eggs. In a third bowl, combine breadcrumbs, paprika, garlic powder, salt, and pepper.
4. Dredge each pickle slice in flour, dip it in the beaten eggs, and coat it with the breadcrumb mixture.
5. Place the coated pickles on the air fryer basket, ensuring they are not touching.
6. Lightly spray the pickles with cooking spray.
7. Air fry for about 10 minutes, flipping halfway through, until the pickles are golden and crispy.
8. Serve the Fried Pickles hot with your favourite dipping sauce.

Melton Mowbray Pork Pie

Prep time: 20 minutes Cook time: 45 minutes Serves 6

Ingredients
- 500g pork sausage meat
- 200g pork shoulder, finely diced
- 1 tablespoon Worcestershire sauce
- Salt and pepper to taste
- 300g all-purpose shortcrust pastry
- 1 egg, beaten (for egg wash)

Instructions
1. Preheat the Ninja Dual Zone Air Fryer to 375°F using the Bake mode.
2. In a bowl, mix together pork sausage meat, diced pork shoulder, Worcestershire sauce, salt, and pepper.
3. Roll out the shortcrust pastry on a floured surface.
4. Cut out circles from the pastry to fit your pie molds.
5. Line the molds with pastry, leaving excess hanging over the edges.
6. Fill each pastry-lined mold with the pork mixture.
7. Fold the excess pastry over the filling, sealing the edges.
8. Brush the pastry with beaten egg for a golden finish.
9. Place the pork pies in the air fryer basket.
10. Bake for about 45 minutes, or until the pastry is golden and the filling is cooked through.
11. Allow to cool slightly before serving.

Bubble and Squeak Scotch Egg Soldiers

Prep time: 30 minutes   Cook time: 20 minutes   Serves 4

Ingredients
- 4 large eggs
- 300g mashed potatoes, cooled
- 200g cabbage, finely shredded
- 1 tablespoon butter
- Salt and pepper to taste
- 100g all-purpose flour
- 2 large eggs, beaten
- 150g breadcrumbs
- Cooking spray

Instructions
1. Preheat the Ninja Dual Zone Air Fryer to 375°F using the Air Fry mode.
2. Boil the eggs for 8 minutes, then cool and peel them.
3. In a skillet, sauté finely shredded cabbage in butter until tender. Mix with cooled mashed potatoes, salt, and pepper.
4. Divide the potato-cabbage mixture into 4 portions.
5. Flatten each portion, encase a boiled egg, and shape into an egg.
6. Roll each scotch egg in flour, dip in beaten egg, and coat with breadcrumbs.
7. Place the scotch eggs in the air fryer basket.
8. Lightly spray the scotch eggs with cooking spray.
9. Air fry for about 20 minutes, turning halfway through, until the scotch eggs are golden and crispy.
10. Serve hot and enjoy.

Cornish Pasty Potato Bites

Prep time: 20 minutes   Cook time: 25 minutes   Serves 4

Ingredients
- 500g potatoes, peeled and diced
- 200g lean beef or lamb, finely diced
- 1 onion, finely chopped
- 1 carrot, grated
- 1 tablespoon olive oil
- Salt and pepper to taste
- 1 pack puff pastry (store-bought or homemade)
- 1 egg, beaten (for egg wash)

Instructions
1. Preheat the Ninja Dual Zone Air Fryer to 375°F using the Bake mode.
2. Boil the diced potatoes until tender, then mash them. Set aside.
3. In a skillet, sauté finely diced beef or lamb, chopped onion, and grated carrot in olive oil until cooked. Season with salt and pepper.
4. Mix the cooked meat mixture with mashed potatoes.
5. Roll out the puff pastry on a floured surface.
6. Cut out circles from the pastry.
7. Place a spoonful of the potato and meat mixture in the center of each pastry circle.
8. Fold the pastry over the filling, creating half-moon shapes. Seal the edges with a fork.
9. Brush each pasty bite with beaten egg.
10. Place the pasty bites on the air fryer basket.
11. Bake for about 20-25 minutes, or until the pastry is golden brown.
12. Serve the Cornish Pasty Potato Bites warm and enjoy with family and friends.

Chicken Liver Pâté Stuffed Mushrooms

Prep time: 15 minutes   Cook time: 15 minutes   Serves 4

Ingredients
- 200g chicken livers, cleaned and trimmed
- 1 onion, finely chopped
- 2 cloves garlic, minced
- 2 tablespoons brandy or cognac
- 2 tablespoons butter
- Salt and pepper to taste
- 8 large mushrooms, cleaned and stems removed

Instructions
1. Preheat the Ninja Dual Zone Air Fryer to 375°F using the Air Fry mode.
2. In a skillet, sauté finely chopped onion and minced garlic in butter until softened.
3. Add chicken livers to the skillet and cook until browned on the outside but slightly pink inside.
4. Deglaze the skillet with brandy or cognac, stirring to incorporate flavours.
5. Transfer the mixture to a food processor and blend until smooth. Season with salt and pepper.
6. Fill each mushroom cap with the chicken liver pâté.
7. Place the stuffed mushrooms on the air fryer basket.
8. Air fry for about 15 minutes, or until the mushrooms are cooked and the pâté is set.
9. Serve warm and enjoy.

Pickled Egg and Bacon Toasted Sandwiches

Prep time: 10 minutes   Cook time: 8 minutes   Serves 2

Ingredients
- 4 slices bread
- 2 pickled eggs, sliced
- 4 slices bacon, cooked
- 4 slices cheddar cheese
- Butter (for spreading)

Instructions
1. Preheat the Ninja Dual Zone Air Fryer to 375°F using the Air Fry mode.
2. Lay out the bread slices.
3. On two slices, layer pickled egg slices, cooked bacon, and cheddar cheese.
4. Place the remaining bread slices on top to form sandwiches.
5. Spread butter on the outer sides of the sandwiches.
6. Place the sandwiches on the air fryer basket.
7. Air fry for about 4 minutes per side, or until the bread is golden and the cheese is melted.
8. Serve your delicious Pickled Egg and Bacon Toasted Sandwiches hot.

Bangers and Mash Croquettes

Prep time: 30 minutes — Cook time: 20 minutes — Serves 4

Ingredients
- 500g mashed potatoes, cooled
- 4 bangers (sausages), cooked and finely chopped
- 1 onion, finely chopped
- 1 tablespoon butter
- Salt and pepper to taste
- 2 eggs, beaten
- Breadcrumbs for coating
- Cooking spray

Instructions
1. Preheat the Ninja Dual Zone Air Fryer to 375°F using the Air Fry mode.
2. In a skillet, sauté finely chopped onion in butter until softened.
3. Mix the sautéed onion, chopped bangers, and mashed potatoes in a bowl. Season with salt and pepper.
4. Shape the mixture into croquettes.
5. Dip each croquette into beaten eggs, then coat with breadcrumbs.
6. Place the croquettes on the air fryer basket.
7. Lightly spray the croquettes with cooking spray.
8. Air fry for about 15-20 minutes, turning halfway through, until the croquettes are golden and crispy.
9. Serve the delicious Bangers and Mash Croquettes hot.

Currywurst Spring Rolls

Prep time: 20 minutes — Cook time: 10 minutes — Serves 4

Ingredients
- 300g bratwurst or German sausage, cooked and sliced
- 227g sauerkraut, drained
- 1 teaspoon curry powder
- 8 spring roll wrappers
- Cooking spray

Instructions
1. Preheat the Ninja Dual Zone Air Fryer to 375°F using the Air Fry mode.
2. In a bowl, mix sliced bratwurst, drained sauerkraut, and curry powder.
3. Place a spoonful of the bratwurst mixture in the center of each spring roll wrapper.
4. Fold in the sides and roll up the spring rolls, sealing the edges with a bit of water.
5. Place the spring rolls on the air fryer basket.
6. Lightly spray the spring rolls with cooking spray.
7. Air fry for about 8-10 minutes, turning halfway through, until the spring rolls are golden and crispy.
8. Serve hot for the best taste.

Chapter 3
Dinner

Stilton and Broccoli Quiche

Prep time: 20 minutes Cook time: 35 minutes Serves 6

Ingredients
- 1 refrigerated pie crust (store-bought or homemade)
- 200g broccoli, blanched and chopped
- 150g Stilton cheese, crumbled
- 1 onion, finely chopped
- 4 large eggs
- 200ml milk
- Salt and pepper to taste
- Fresh chives (for garnish)

Instructions
1. Preheat the Ninja Dual Zone Air Fryer to 375°F using the Bake mode.
2. Roll out the pie crust and line a pie dish with it.
3. In a skillet, sauté finely chopped onion until translucent.
4. In a bowl, whisk together eggs and milk. Season with salt and pepper.
5. Spread the sautéed onions, chopped broccoli, and crumbled Stilton cheese evenly over the pie crust.
6. Pour the egg and milk mixture over the filling.
7. Bake in the air fryer for about 30-35 minutes or until the quiche is set and golden brown.
8. Garnish with fresh chives.
9. Allow to cool slightly before slicing and serving.

Scampi and Chips

Prep time: 15 minutes Cook time: 15 minutes Serves 2

Ingredients
- 200g scampi or large shrimp, peeled and deveined
- 120g breadcrumbs
- 1 egg, beaten
- Cooking spray
- 400g potatoes, cut into fries
- Salt and pepper to taste

Instructions
1. Preheat the Ninja Dual Zone Air Fryer to 375°F using the Air Fry mode.
2. Dip scampi or shrimp in beaten egg, then coat with breadcrumbs.
3. Place the coated scampi in the air fryer basket. Lightly spray with cooking spray.
4. In a separate basket, toss potato fries with a bit of oil, salt, and pepper.
5. Air fry the scampi for about 8-10 minutes, until golden and crispy.
6. Simultaneously, air fry the potato fries for about 15-20 minutes, or until they are golden and cooked through.
7. Serve your wholesome Scampi and Chips meal hot for the best dinner time.

Lamb Kofta Kebabs

Prep time: 20 minutes　　　Cook time: 12 minutes　　　Serves 4

Ingredients
- 500g ground lamb
- 1 onion, grated
- 2 cloves garlic, minced
- 1 teaspoon ground cumin
- 1 teaspoon ground coriander
- 1/2 teaspoon paprika
- Salt and pepper to taste
- Fresh mint leaves (for garnish)
- Greek yoghourt (for dipping)

Instructions
1. Preheat the Ninja Dual Zone Air Fryer to 375°F using the Air Fry mode.
2. In a bowl, combine ground lamb, grated onion, minced garlic, ground cumin, ground coriander, paprika, salt, and pepper.
3. Divide the mixture and shape it onto skewers to form kebabs.
4. Place the lamb kofta kebabs on the air fryer basket.
5. Air fry for about 12 minutes, turning occasionally, until they are cooked through and have a nice char.
6. Garnish with fresh mint leaves.
7. Serve hot with a side of Greek yoghourt for dipping.

Pheasant with Cranberry Sauce

Prep time: 15 minutes　　　Cook time: 30 minutes　　　Serves 4

Ingredients
- 4 pheasant breasts
- Salt and pepper to taste
- 200g cranberries
- 100g sugar
- 1 orange, zest and juice
- 1 tablespoon olive oil
- Fresh thyme (for garnish)

Instructions
1. Preheat the Ninja Dual Zone Air Fryer to 375°F using the Roast mode.
2. Season pheasant breasts with salt and pepper.
3. In a saucepan, combine cranberries, sugar, orange zest, and juice. Simmer until cranberries burst and sauce thickens.
4. In a separate skillet, heat olive oil and sear pheasant breasts until golden brown.
5. Transfer the pheasant to the air fryer basket and roast for about 20-25 minutes or until cooked through.
6. Serve pheasant with cranberry sauce, garnished with fresh thyme.

Chicken Fajitas and chips

Prep time: 20 minutes   Cook time: 15 minutes   Serves 4

Ingredients
- 500g chicken breast, sliced
- 1 bell pepper, sliced
- 1 onion, sliced
- 2 tablespoons fajita seasoning
- 1 tablespoon olive oil
- 400g tortilla chips

Instructions
1. Preheat the Ninja Dual Zone Air Fryer to 375°F using the Air Fry mode.
2. In a bowl, toss chicken, bell pepper, onion, fajita seasoning, and olive oil.
3. Spread the mixture on one side of the air fryer basket.
4. Air fry for about 10-15 minutes or until chicken is cooked and veggies are tender.
5. In the other basket, air fry tortilla chips until golden.
6. Serve Chicken Fajitas and Chips hot with your favourite toppings.

Mexican Chicken and Sweet Potatoes

Prep time: 15 minutes   Cook time: 30 minutes   Serves 4

Ingredients
- 4 boneless, skinless chicken parts of your choice
- 2 sweet potatoes, peeled and diced
- 1 can black beans, drained and rinsed
- 160g corn kernels
- 1 teaspoon cumin
- 1 teaspoon chilli powder
- Salt and pepper to taste
- 2 tablespoons olive oil
- Fresh cilantro (for garnish)

Instructions
1. Preheat the Ninja Dual Zone Air Fryer to 375°F using the Roast mode.
2. Season chicken with cumin, chilli powder, salt, and pepper.
3. In a bowl, toss sweet potatoes, black beans, and corn with olive oil.
4. Place chicken on one side of the air fryer basket and sweet potato mixture on the other.
5. Roast for about 25-30 minutes or until chicken is cooked through and sweet potatoes are tender.
6. Garnish with fresh cilantro before serving.

Nando's Loaded Chicken Chips

Prep time: 20 minutes | Cook time: 30 minutes | Serves 4

Ingredients
- 500g skin-on fries
- 400g cooked chicken, shredded
- 100g cheddar cheese, shredded
- 120ml Nando's Peri-Peri sauce
- Green onions (for garnish)
- Sour cream (for dipping)

Instructions
1. Preheat the Ninja Dual Zone Air Fryer to 375°F using the Air Fry mode.
2. Cook skin-on fries in the air fryer until golden and crispy.
3. In a large bowl, toss the cooked fries with shredded chicken, cheddar cheese, and Nando's Peri-Peri sauce.
4. Transfer the loaded fries mixture back to the air fryer basket and air fry for an additional 5-7 minutes, or until the cheese is melted.
5. Garnish with chopped green onions.
6. Serve the Nando's Loaded Chicken Chips hot with a side of sour cream for dipping.
7. Enjoy this flavourful and indulgent dish inspired by Nando's.

Tikka Chicken Salad with Popadoms

Prep time: 15 minutes | Cook time: 10 minutes | Serves 2

Ingredients
- 300g chicken breast, diced
- 2 tablespoons tikka masala paste
- 120g mixed salad greens
- 1 cucumber, sliced
- 240ml cherry tomatoes, halved
- 4 popadoms, cooked
- Yoghurt dressing (optional)

Instructions
1. Preheat the Ninja Dual Zone Air Fryer to 375°F using the Air Fry mode.
2. In a bowl, toss diced chicken with tikka masala paste until well coated.
3. Air fry the marinated chicken for about 8-10 minutes or until cooked through.
4. In a large salad bowl, combine mixed greens, sliced cucumber, and cherry tomatoes.
5. Top the salad with air-fried tikka chicken.
6. Serve the Tikka Chicken Salad with Popadoms with cooked poppadoms on the side.
7. Drizzle with yoghurt dressing if desired.

Peri Peri Chicken Wraps and Chips

Prep time: 25 minutes Cook time: 20 minutes Serves 4

Ingredients
- 500g chicken breast, sliced
- 120ml Nando's Peri-Peri sauce
- 4 whole wheat wraps
- 240ml lettuce, shredded
- 1 tomato, diced
- 120ml cucumber, sliced
- 1/2 red onion, thinly sliced
- Greek yoghurt or tzatziki (optional)
- 400g potato wedges (for chips)

Instructions
1. Preheat the Ninja Dual Zone Air Fryer to 375°F using the Air Fry mode.
2. Marinate sliced chicken breast in Nando's Peri-Peri sauce for at least 15 minutes.
3. Air fry marinated chicken slices until cooked through and slightly charred.
4. Warm whole wheat wraps in the air fryer for a few seconds.
5. Assemble wraps with shredded lettuce, diced tomato, sliced cucumber, and thinly sliced red onion.
6. Place cooked peri peri chicken in each wrap.
7. Drizzle with Greek yoghurt or tzatziki if desired.
8. Serve Peri Peri Chicken Wraps with a side of crispy potato wedges.
9. Enjoy this delicious and spicy meal.

Garlic Parmesan Carrot Fries

Prep time: 15 minutes Cook time: 20 minutes Serves 4

Ingredients
- 500g carrots, cut into fries
- 2 tablespoons olive oil
- 3 cloves garlic, minced
- 30g Parmesan cheese, grated
- Salt and pepper to taste
- Fresh parsley (for garnish)

Instructions
1. Preheat the Ninja Dual Zone Air Fryer to 375°F using the Air Fry mode.
2. In a bowl, toss carrot fries with olive oil, minced garlic, Parmesan cheese, salt, and pepper.
3. Spread the seasoned carrot fries in the air fryer basket.
4. Air fry for about 15-20 minutes or until the carrot fries are golden and crispy.
5. Garnish with fresh parsley.
6. Serve the Garlic Parmesan Carrot Fries hot as a tasty and healthier alternative to regular fries.

Honey Mustard Glazed Pork Tenderloin

Prep time: 15 minutes   Cook time: 25 minutes   Serves 4

Ingredients
- 2 pork tenderloins
- Salt and pepper to taste
- 60g Dijon mustard
- 30g honey
- 30g whole grain mustard
- 2 cloves garlic, minced
- 15ml olive oil
- Fresh parsley (for garnish)

Instructions
1. Preheat the Ninja Dual Zone Air Fryer to 375°F using the Roast mode.
2. Season pork tenderloins with salt and pepper.
3. In a bowl, mix together Dijon mustard, honey, whole grain mustard, minced garlic, and olive oil.
4. Brush the honey mustard glaze over the pork tenderloins.
5. Place the tenderloins in the air fryer basket and roast for about 20-25 minutes or until the internal temperature reaches 145°F.
6. Baste the pork with the glaze halfway through the cooking time.
7. Garnish with fresh parsley.
8. Let the Honey Mustard Glazed Pork Tenderloin rest for a few minutes before slicing.
9. Serve and enjoy.

Lemon Herb Roast Chicken

Prep time: 20 minutes   Cook time: 40 minutes   Serves 4

Ingredients
- 1 whole chicken (about 1.5kg)
- Salt and pepper to taste
- 2 lemons, sliced
- 4 cloves garlic, minced
- 2 tablespoons fresh rosemary, chopped
- 2 tablespoons fresh thyme, chopped
- 15ml olive oil

Instructions
1. Preheat the Ninja Dual Zone Air Fryer to 375°F using the Roast mode.
2. Season the whole chicken with salt and pepper, inside and out.
3. Place lemon slices and minced garlic inside the chicken cavity.
4. In a bowl, mix together chopped rosemary, thyme, and olive oil.
5. Rub the herb mixture over the chicken, ensuring it's evenly coated.
6. Place the chicken in the air fryer basket and roast for about 35-40 minutes or until the internal temperature reaches 165°F.
7. Baste the chicken with its juices halfway through the cooking time.
8. Let the Lemon Herb Roast Chicken rest for a few minutes before carving.
9. Serve and enjoy this aromatic and juicy roast chicken

Pesto Chicken Pasta

Prep time: 15 minutes   Cook time: 20 minutes   Serves 4

Ingredients
- 400g boneless, skinless chicken breasts, sliced
- Salt and pepper to taste
- 250g pasta of your choice
- 250g cherry tomatoes, halved
- 125g pesto sauce
- 30g Parmesan cheese, grated
- Fresh basil (for garnish)

Instructions
1. Preheat the Ninja Dual Zone Air Fryer to 375°F using the Bake mode.
2. Season chicken slices with salt and pepper.
3. Cook pasta according to package instructions; drain.
4. In a pan, cook chicken slices until no longer pink.
5. In a large bowl, combine cooked pasta, cooked chicken, cherry tomatoes, pesto sauce, and Parmesan cheese.
6. Transfer the mixture to a baking dish.
7. Bake for about 15-20 minutes or until heated through.
8. Garnish with fresh basil before serving.
9. Enjoy your delightful Pesto Chicken Pasta.

Baked Cod with Herbed Breadcrumbs

Prep time: 15 minutes   Cook time: 20 minutes   Serves 4

Ingredients
- 4 cod fillets (about 150g each)
- Salt and pepper to taste
- 115g breadcrumbs
- 2 tablespoons fresh parsley, chopped
- 1 tablespoon fresh dill, chopped
- 1 tablespoon lemon zest
- 2 tablespoons olive oil

Instructions
1. Preheat the Ninja Dual Zone Air Fryer to 375°F using the Bake mode.
2. Season cod fillets with salt and pepper.
3. In a bowl, combine breadcrumbs, chopped parsley, chopped dill, and lemon zest.
4. Brush cod fillets with olive oil, then coat with the herbed breadcrumb mixture.
5. Place the coated cod fillets in the air fryer basket.
6. Bake for about 15-20 minutes or until the cod is cooked through and the breadcrumbs are golden brown.
7. Serve the Baked Cod with Herbed Breadcrumbs hot, garnished with additional fresh herbs if desired.

Salmon en Papillote

Prep time: 15 minutes   Cook time: 20 minutes   Serves 4

Ingredients
- 4 salmon fillets (about 150g each)
- Salt and pepper to taste
- Cherry tomatoes, halved
- Asparagus, trimmed
- Lemon slices
- Fresh dill sprigs
- 30ml olive oil
- Parchment paper sheets

Instructions
1. Preheat the Ninja Dual Zone Air Fryer to 375°F using the Bake mode.
2. Season salmon fillets with salt and pepper.
3. Place each salmon fillet on a sheet of parchment paper.
4. Divide cherry tomatoes and asparagus evenly among the salmon fillets.
5. Drizzle each fillet with olive oil and top with a slice of lemon and a sprig of fresh dill.
6. Fold the parchment paper over the salmon and vegetables, sealing the edges to create a packet.
7. Place the packets in the air fryer basket.
8. Bake for about 15-20 minutes or until the salmon is cooked through and the vegetables are tender.
9. Carefully open the packets and transfer the Salmon en Papillote to plates then serve.

Chicken Parmesan

Prep time: 15 minutes   Cook time: 25 minutes   Serves 4

Ingredients
- 4 boneless, skinless chicken breasts (about 150g each)
- Salt and pepper to taste
- 115g breadcrumbs
- 60g grated Parmesan cheese
- 480ml marinara sauce
- 120g shredded mozzarella cheese
- Fresh basil (for garnish)

Instructions
1. Preheat the Ninja Dual Zone Air Fryer to 375°F using the Bake mode.
2. Season chicken breasts with salt and pepper.
3. In a bowl, combine breadcrumbs and grated Parmesan cheese.
4. Coat each chicken breast with the breadcrumb mixture.
5. Place the coated chicken breasts in the air fryer basket.
6. Bake for about 20-25 minutes or until the chicken is cooked through and the coating is crispy.
7. Spoon marinara sauce over each chicken breast.
8. Sprinkle shredded mozzarella cheese on top.
9. Continue baking for an additional 5 minutes or until the cheese is melted and bubbly.
10. Garnish with fresh basil before serving.

Stuffed Bell Peppers

Prep time: 20 minutes   Cook time: 30 minutes   Serves 4

Ingredients
- 4 large bell peppers
- 200g lean ground beef
- 200g cooked rice
- 240g black beans, drained and rinsed
- 160g corn kernels
- 240g diced tomatoes
- 120g shredded cheddar cheese
- 1 teaspoon chilli powder
- Salt and pepper to taste
- Fresh cilantro (for garnish)

Instructions
1. Preheat the Ninja Dual Zone Air Fryer to 375°F using the Bake mode.
2. Cut the tops off the bell peppers and remove seeds and membranes.
3. In a skillet, brown ground beef over medium heat; drain excess fat.
4. In a bowl, combine cooked beef, rice, black beans, corn, diced tomatoes, shredded cheddar cheese, chilli powder, salt, and pepper.
5. Stuff each bell pepper with the mixture and place them in the air fryer basket.
6. Bake for about 25-30 minutes or until the peppers are tender.
7. Garnish with fresh cilantro before serving.

Teriyaki Salmon

Prep time: 15 minutes   Cook time: 20 minutes   Serves 4

Ingredients
- 4 salmon fillets (about 150g each)
- 120ml soy sauce
- 60ml mirin
- 30g brown sugar
- 2 cloves garlic, minced
- 15ml ginger, grated
- 30ml sesame oil
- Green onions (for garnish)

Instructions
1. Preheat the Ninja Dual Zone Air Fryer to 375°F using the Bake mode.
2. In a bowl, mix soy sauce, mirin, brown sugar, minced garlic, grated ginger, and sesame oil to create the teriyaki sauce.
3. Place salmon fillets in a dish and pour half of the teriyaki sauce over them. Marinate for 10 minutes.
4. Remove salmon from the marinade and place in the air fryer basket.
5. Bake for about 15-20 minutes or until the salmon is cooked through, brushing with the remaining teriyaki sauce halfway through.
6. Garnish with green onions before serving.
7. Enjoy this delicious Teriyaki Salmon with family and friends.

Chapter 4
Beef, Pork and Lamb

Beef and Ale Baked Beans

Prep time: 15 minutes Cook time: 40 minutes Serves 4

Ingredients
- 400g canned baked beans
- 200g cooked beef, diced
- 1 onion, finely chopped
- 2 cloves garlic, minced
- 120ml ale
- 2 tablespoons tomato paste
- 1 tablespoon brown sugar
- 1 tablespoon Worcestershire sauce
- Salt and pepper to taste
- Fresh parsley (for garnish)

Instructions
1. Preheat the Ninja Dual Zone Air Fryer to 375°F using the Bake mode.
2. In a pan, sauté chopped onion and minced garlic until softened.
3. Add diced beef to the pan and cook until browned.
4. Pour in ale, baked beans, tomato paste, brown sugar, and Worcestershire sauce.
5. Season with salt and pepper. Stir well.
6. Transfer the mixture to a baking dish and place it in the air fryer basket.
7. Bake for about 30-40 minutes or until the beans are bubbling and the top is golden.
8. Garnish with fresh parsley before serving.

Pork and Black Pudding Roulade

Prep time: 20 minutes Cook time: 35 minutes Serves 4

Ingredients
- 500g pork tenderloin
- 200g black pudding, crumbled
- 1 apple, grated
- 1 tablespoon wholegrain mustard
- Salt and pepper to taste
- 2 tablespoons olive oil

Instructions
1. Preheat the Ninja Dual Zone Air Fryer to 375°F using the Bake mode.
2. Butterfly the pork tenderloin and flatten it with a meat mallet.
3. Season the pork with salt and pepper.
4. In a bowl, mix crumbled black pudding, grated apple, and wholegrain mustard.
5. Spread the black pudding mixture over the pork.
6. Roll the pork into a roulade and secure with kitchen twine.
7. Brush the roulade with olive oil and place it in the air fryer basket.
8. Bake for about 30-35 minutes or until the pork is cooked through.
9. Let it rest for a few minutes before slicing.
10. Serve your delicious Pork and Black Pudding Roulade for a delicious meal.

Lamb and Apricot Tagine

Prep time: 20 minutes | Cook time: 1 hour | Serves 4

Ingredients
- 500g lamb, cubed
- 1 onion, finely chopped
- 2 cloves garlic, minced
- 1 teaspoon ground cumin
- 1 teaspoon ground coriander
- 1 teaspoon ground cinnamon
- 1/2 teaspoon ground ginger
- 400g canned diced tomatoes
- 250ml chicken broth
- 150g dried apricots, halved
- 2 tablespoons honey
- Salt and pepper to taste
- Fresh cilantro (for garnish)

Instructions
1. Preheat the Ninja Dual Zone Air Fryer to 375°F using the Bake mode.
2. In a pan, brown lamb cubes until seared. Set aside.
3. In the same pan, sauté chopped onion and minced garlic until softened.
4. Add ground cumin, ground coriander, ground cinnamon, and ground ginger to the pan. Stir well.
5. Pour in diced tomatoes, chicken broth, honey, and season with salt and pepper. Bring to a simmer.
6. Add seared lamb and dried apricots to the pan. Stir to combine.
7. Transfer the mixture to a tagine or a baking dish and place it in the air fryer basket.
8. Bake for about 50-60 minutes or until the lamb is tender.
9. Garnish with fresh cilantro before serving.
10. Enjoy the rich flavours of Lamb and Apricot Tagine.

Filipino Fried Pork (Pritong Baboy)

Prep time: 15 minutes | Cook time: 20 minutes | Serves 4

Ingredients
- 500g pork belly, sliced
- 3 cloves garlic, minced
- 1 tablespoon soy sauce
- 1 tablespoon vinegar
- 1 teaspoon salt
- 1/2 teaspoon black pepper
- Cooking oil for air frying

Instructions
1. Preheat the Ninja Dual Zone Air Fryer to 375°F using the Air Fry mode.
2. In a bowl, marinate pork slices with minced garlic, soy sauce, vinegar, salt, and black pepper.
3. Arrange the marinated pork slices in the air fryer basket.
4. Air fry for about 15-20 minutes or until the pork is crispy and cooked through.
5. Serve the Filipino Fried Pork hot and enjoy this flavourful dish!

Cajun Pork Fillet with Sweet Potatoes

Prep time: 20 minutes   Cook time: 40 minutes   Serves 4

Ingredients
- 500g pork fillet
- 2 sweet potatoes, peeled and cubed
- 1 tablespoon Cajun seasoning
- 2 tablespoons olive oil
- 1 teaspoon paprika
- 1 teaspoon garlic powder
- Salt and pepper to taste
- Fresh parsley (for garnish)

Instructions
1. Preheat the Ninja Dual Zone Air Fryer to 375°F using the Bake mode.
2. Rub pork fillet with Cajun seasoning, paprika, garlic powder, salt, and pepper.
3. In a bowl, toss cubed sweet potatoes with olive oil, salt, and pepper.
4. Place the seasoned pork fillet and sweet potatoes in the air fryer basket.
5. Bake for about 35-40 minutes or until the pork is cooked through and sweet potatoes are tender.
6. Garnish with fresh parsley before serving.

Tikka Pork Chops

Prep time: 15 minutes   Cook time: 25 minutes   Serves 4

Ingredients
- 4 pork chops (about 150g each)
- 120g plain yoghurt
- 2 tablespoons tikka masala paste
- 1 teaspoon ground cumin
- 1 teaspoon ground coriander
- 1 teaspoon garam masala
- Salt and pepper to taste
- Lemon wedges (for serving)

Instructions
1. Preheat the Ninja Dual Zone Air Fryer to 375°F using the Air Fry mode.
2. In a bowl, mix plain yoghurt, tikka masala paste, ground cumin, ground coriander, garam masala, salt, and pepper.
3. Coat pork chops with the marinade and let them sit for 10-15 minutes.
4. Place marinated pork chops in the air fryer basket.
5. Air fry for about 20-25 minutes or until the pork is cooked through and has a golden exterior.
6. Serve with lemon wedges for a burst of freshness.

Beef and Tattie Scones

Prep time: 20 minutes Cook time: 30 minutes Serves 4

Ingredients
- 300g minced beef
- 4 large potatoes, boiled and mashed
- 1 onion, finely chopped
- 1 teaspoon dried thyme
- Salt and pepper to taste
- 2 tablespoons vegetable oil

Instructions
1. Preheat the Ninja Dual Zone Air Fryer to 375°F using the Bake mode.
2. In a pan, sauté finely chopped onion until softened.
3. Add minced beef and cook until browned.
4. Stir in dried thyme, salt, and pepper to the beef mixture.
5. In a bowl, combine the mashed potatoes with the seasoned beef mixture.
6. Form the mixture into scone-shaped patties.
7. Brush each scone with vegetable oil and place them in the air fryer basket.
8. Bake for about 25-30 minutes or until the scones are golden brown.
9. Serve warm and enjoy!

Pork and Chorizo Cassoulet

Prep time: 25 minutes Cook time: 40 minutes Serves 4

Ingredients
- 500g pork shoulder, cubed
- 150g chorizo, sliced
- 1 onion, finely chopped
- 2 cloves garlic, minced
- 2 carrots, diced
- 1 can (400g) cannellini beans, drained and rinsed
- 250ml chicken broth
- 2 tablespoons tomato paste
- 1 teaspoon dried thyme
- Salt and pepper to taste
- Fresh parsley (for garnish)

Instructions
1. Preheat the Ninja Dual Zone Air Fryer to 375°F using the Bake mode.
2. In a pan, brown cubed pork shoulder until seared. Set aside.
3. In the same pan, sauté finely chopped onion and minced garlic until softened.
4. Add sliced chorizo, diced carrots, cannellini beans, chicken broth, tomato paste, dried thyme, salt, and pepper. Stir well.
5. Transfer the mixture to a baking dish and place it in the air fryer basket.
6. Bake for about 35-40 minutes or until the cassoulet is bubbling and the top is golden.
7. Garnish with fresh parsley before serving.

Lamb and Roasted Pepper Quiche

Prep time: 25 minutes Cook time: 40 minutes Serves 4

Ingredients
- 1 ready-made pie crust
- 200g lamb, cooked and shredded
- 1 red bell pepper, roasted and sliced
- 1 yellow bell pepper, roasted and sliced
- 1 onion, caramelised
- 150g feta cheese, crumbled
- 4 eggs
- 200ml milk
- Salt and pepper to taste
- Fresh parsley (for garnish)

Instructions
1. Preheat the Ninja Dual Zone Air Fryer to 375°F using the Bake mode.
2. Line a pie dish with the ready-made pie crust.
3. In a bowl, whisk together eggs, milk, salt, and pepper.
4. Spread shredded lamb, roasted red and yellow bell peppers, caramelised onion, and crumbled feta cheese over the pie crust.
5. Pour the egg mixture over the filling.
6. Place the quiche in the air fryer basket.
7. Bake for about 35-40 minutes or until the quiche is set and golden.
8. Garnish with fresh parsley before serving.

Lamb and caramelised Onion Gravy

Prep time: 20 minutes Cook time: 30 minutes Serves 4

Ingredients
- 500g lamb chops
- 2 onions, thinly sliced
- 2 tablespoons olive oil
- 2 tablespoons all-purpose flour
- 500ml beef broth
- 2 tablespoons balsamic vinegar
- 1 tablespoon brown sugar
- Salt and pepper to taste

Instructions
1. Preheat the Ninja Dual Zone Air Fryer to 375°F using the Bake mode.
2. Season lamb chops with salt and pepper.
3. In a pan, sear lamb chops until browned on both sides. Set aside.
4. In the same pan, sauté thinly sliced onions in olive oil until caramelised.
5. Sprinkle flour over the caramelised onions and stir to create a roux.
6. Gradually add beef broth, balsamic vinegar, and brown sugar to the pan. Stir until the gravy thickens.
7. Return seared lamb chops to the pan and coat them with the caramelised onion gravy.
8. Transfer the lamb and gravy to a baking dish and place it in the air fryer basket.
9. Bake for about 25-30 minutes or until the lamb is cooked through.
10. Serve the Lamb and Caramelised Onion Gravy hot.

Lamb and Tomato Tarts

Prep time: 25 minutes   Cook time: 30 minutes   Serves 4

Ingredients
- 1 sheet puff pastry, thawed
- 200g cooked lamb, shredded
- 75g cherry tomatoes, halved
- 100g feta cheese, crumbled
- 1 tablespoon olive oil
- Fresh basil leaves (for garnish)
- Salt and pepper to taste

Instructions
1. Preheat the Ninja Dual Zone Air Fryer to 375°F using the Bake mode.
2. Roll out the puff pastry and cut it into individual tart-sized squares.
3. Place the pastry squares on a baking sheet.
4. In a bowl, mix shredded lamb, cherry tomatoes, feta cheese, olive oil, salt, and pepper.
5. Spoon the lamb and tomato mixture onto each pastry square.
6. Place the tarts in the air fryer basket.
7. Bake for about 25-30 minutes or until the pastry is golden and the filling is heated through.
8. Garnish with fresh basil leaves before serving.

Beef and Horseradish Suet Pudding

Prep time: 30 minutes   Cook time: 1 hour 15 minutes   Serves 4

Ingredients
- 400g beef stewing meat, cubed
- 1 onion, finely chopped
- 2 carrots, diced
- 2 tablespoons horseradish sauce
- 300g self-raising flour
- 150g suet
- 150ml water
- Salt and pepper to taste

Instructions
1. Preheat the Ninja Dual Zone Air Fryer to 375°F using the Bake mode.
2. In a pan, brown beef cubes until seared. Set aside.
3. In the same pan, sauté finely chopped onion and diced carrots until softened.
4. Mix horseradish sauce into the beef and vegetable mixture. Season with salt and pepper.
5. In a bowl, combine self-raising flour, suet, and water to form a dough.
6. Roll out the dough on a floured surface and line a greased pudding basin.
7. Spoon the beef and vegetable mixture into the pudding basin.
8. Cover with a suet pastry lid and seal the edges.
9. Place the pudding basin in the air fryer basket.
10. Bake for about 1 hour and 15 minutes or until the suet pudding is cooked through and golden.
11. Serve your Beef and Horseradish Suet Pudding hot and enjoy the comforting flavours.

Chapter 5
Fish and Seafood

Bass with Sauce Vierge

Prep time: 15 minutes | Cook time: 20 minutes | Serves 4

Ingredients
- 4 bass fillets
- 2 tablespoons olive oil
- 2 tablespoons fresh lemon juice
- 2 tomatoes, diced
- 1 shallot, finely chopped
- 1 clove garlic, minced
- 2 tablespoons fresh basil, chopped
- 1 tablespoon capers, drained
- Salt and pepper to taste

Instructions
1. Preheat the Ninja Dual Zone Air Fryer to 375°F using the Bake mode.
2. Place bass fillets on a baking tray.
3. Drizzle olive oil and lemon juice over the fillets, then season with salt and pepper.
4. In a bowl, combine diced tomatoes, chopped shallot, minced garlic, fresh basil, and capers to create the Sauce Vierge.
5. Spoon the Sauce Vierge over the bass fillets.
6. Bake for about 15-20 minutes or until the fish is cooked through and flakes easily.
7. Serve your yummy Bass with Sauce Vierge hot, and enjoy the vibrant flavours.

Monkfish with Parma Ham

Prep time: 20 minutes | Cook time: 25 minutes | Serves 4

Ingredients
- 4 monkfish fillets
- 4 slices Parma ham
- 2 tablespoons olive oil
- 1 lemon, zest and juice
- 2 tablespoons fresh parsley, chopped
- Salt and pepper to taste

Instructions
1. Preheat the Ninja Dual Zone Air Fryer to 375°F using the Bake mode.
2. Wrap each monkfish fillet with a slice of Parma ham.
3. Drizzle olive oil over the wrapped fillets and season with salt and pepper.
4. Place the fillets on a baking tray.
5. Sprinkle lemon zest and juice over the fillets and top with chopped fresh parsley.
6. Bake for about 20-25 minutes or until the monkfish is cooked through and Parma ham is crispy.
7. Serve the Monkfish with Parma Ham hot, and relish the delicious combination!

Lobster and Scallop Thermidor

Prep time: 25 minutes Cook time: 20 minutes Serves 4

Ingredients
- 2 lobster tails, cooked and meat removed
- 8 large scallops
- 2 tablespoons unsalted butter
- 2 tablespoons all-purpose flour
- 200ml whole milk
- 50g Gruyere cheese, grated
- 2 tablespoons Dijon mustard
- 2 tablespoons fresh tarragon, chopped
- Salt and pepper to taste

Instructions
1. Preheat the Ninja Dual Zone Air Fryer to 375°F using the Bake mode.
2. Slice lobster meat and arrange it with scallops in a baking dish.
3. In a saucepan, melt butter, add flour, and cook to form a roux.
4. Gradually whisk in milk until the mixture thickens.
5. Add grated Gruyere cheese, Dijon mustard, chopped tarragon, salt, and pepper. Stir until the cheese is melted.
6. Pour the sauce over lobster and scallops in the baking dish.
7. Bake for about 15-20 minutes or until the top is golden and bubbly.
8. Serve the Lobster and Scallop Thermidor hot for the best family time.

Monkfish Cheeks

Prep time: 15 minutes Cook time: 10 minutes Serves 4

Ingredients
- 500g monkfish cheeks
- 2 tablespoons olive oil
- 1 lemon, zest and juice
- 2 cloves garlic, minced
- 1 tablespoon fresh parsley, chopped
- Salt and pepper to taste

Instructions
1. Preheat the Ninja Dual Zone Air Fryer to 375°F using the Bake mode.
2. In a bowl, toss monkfish cheeks with olive oil, lemon zest, lemon juice, minced garlic, and chopped fresh parsley.
3. Season with salt and pepper.
4. Arrange the monkfish cheeks on a baking tray.
5. Bake for about 8-10 minutes or until the cheeks are cooked through and lightly browned.
6. Serve hot, and enjoy the succulent flavours.

Mussels in Cider

Prep time: 15 minutes | Cook time: 15 minutes | Serves 4

Ingredients
- 1000g fresh mussels, cleaned and debearded
- 2 tablespoons olive oil
- 1 onion, finely chopped
- 2 cloves garlic, minced
- 200ml dry cider
- 100ml heavy cream
- 1 tablespoon fresh thyme leaves
- Salt and pepper to taste

Instructions
1. Preheat the Ninja Dual Zone Air Fryer to 375°F using the Bake mode.
2. In a large pan, heat olive oil and sauté chopped onion and minced garlic until softened.
3. Add cleaned mussels to the pan.
4. Pour in dry cider and heavy cream.
5. Sprinkle fresh thyme leaves over the mussels and season with salt and pepper.
6. Transfer the mussels and cider mixture to a baking dish.
7. Bake for about 10-15 minutes or until the mussels are open and cooked.
8. Best served hot.

Sea Bass with Fennel and Blood Orange

Prep time: 20 minutes | Cook time: 20 minutes | Serves 4

Ingredients
- 4 sea bass fillets
- 2 tablespoons olive oil
- 1 fennel bulb, thinly sliced
- 2 blood oranges, peeled and segmented
- 1 tablespoon fresh thyme leaves
- Salt and pepper to taste

Instructions
1. Preheat the Ninja Dual Zone Air Fryer to 375°F using the Bake mode.
2. Rub sea bass fillets with olive oil and season with salt and pepper.
3. Scatter sliced fennel and blood orange segments on a baking tray.
4. Place sea bass fillets on top of the fennel and oranges.
5. Sprinkle fresh thyme leaves over the fillets.
6. Bake for about 15-20 minutes or until the sea bass is cooked through and flakes easily.
7. Serve hot and enjoy

Hake and Chorizo Stew

Prep time: 20 minutes   Cook time: 30 minutes   Serves 4

Ingredients
- 500g hake fillets, cut into chunks
- 100g chorizo, sliced
- 1 onion, finely chopped
- 2 cloves garlic, minced
- 1 red bell pepper, diced
- 1 can (400g) diced tomatoes
- 200ml fish stock
- 1 teaspoon smoked paprika
- 1 teaspoon dried oregano
- Salt and pepper to taste
- Fresh parsley, chopped (for garnish)

Instructions
1. Preheat the Ninja Dual Zone Air Fryer to 375°F using the Bake mode.
2. In a large pan, sauté chorizo slices until they release their oils.
3. Add finely chopped onion and minced garlic, cooking until softened.
4. Stir in diced tomatoes, fish stock, smoked paprika, and dried oregano.
5. Bring the stew to a simmer, then add hake chunks and diced red bell pepper.
6. Season with salt and pepper, and transfer the mixture to a baking dish.
7. Bake for about 25-30 minutes or until the hake is cooked through.
8. Garnish the Hake and Chorizo Stew with chopped fresh parsley before serving.

Grilled Sardines

Prep time: 15 minutes   Cook time: 10 minutes   Serves 4

Ingredients
- 8 fresh sardines, cleaned and gutted
- 2 tablespoons olive oil
- 2 cloves garlic, minced
- 1 lemon, sliced
- Fresh parsley, chopped (for garnish)
- Salt and pepper to taste

Instructions
1. Preheat the Ninja Dual Zone Air Fryer to 400°F using the Grill mode.
2. Make diagonal cuts on each side of the sardines.
3. Mix olive oil and minced garlic, then brush the mixture onto the sardines.
4. Season the sardines with salt and pepper.
5. Place the sardines on the grill rack.
6. Grill for about 4-5 minutes per side or until the skin is crispy and the flesh is cooked.
7. Garnish the Grilled Sardines with lemon slices and chopped fresh parsley before serving.

Plaice Goujons

Prep time: 15 minutes | Cook time: 15 minutes | Serves 4

Ingredients
- 500g plaice fillets, cut into strips
- 250g breadcrumbs
- 2 eggs, beaten
- 1 lemon, zest and juice
- 2 tablespoons fresh parsley, chopped
- Salt and pepper to taste
- Tartar sauce (for dipping)

Instructions
1. Preheat the Ninja Dual Zone Air Fryer to 375°F using the Bake mode.
2. Dip plaice strips into beaten eggs, then coat with breadcrumbs.
3. Arrange the coated plaice strips on a baking tray.
4. Sprinkle lemon zest, lemon juice, and chopped fresh parsley over the strips.
5. Bake for about 12-15 minutes or until the plaice is golden and crispy.
6. Serve the Plaice Goujons with tartar sauce for a delightful and crunchy seafood treat.

Tuna Nicoise Salad

Prep time: 20 minutes | Cook time: 10 minutes | Serves 4

Ingredients
- 4 tuna steaks
- 30ml olive oil
- Salt and pepper to taste
- 240g mixed salad greens
- 200g cherry tomatoes, halved
- 200g green beans, blanched
- 4 hard-boiled eggs, sliced
- 100g black olives
- 60ml balsamic vinaigrette

Instructions
1. Preheat the Ninja Dual Zone Air Fryer to 400°F using the Grill mode.
2. Brush tuna steaks with olive oil and season with salt and pepper.
3. Grill tuna steaks for about 3-4 minutes per side or until cooked to your liking.
4. In a large bowl, arrange mixed salad greens, cherry tomatoes, blanched green beans, sliced hard-boiled eggs, and black olives.
5. Place grilled tuna steaks on top of the salad.
6. Drizzle the Tuna Nicoise Salad with balsamic vinaigrette.
7. Serve the salad immediately for a fresh and flavourful meal.

Skate with Black Butter

Prep time: 15 minutes Cook time: 10 minutes Serves 4

Ingredients
- 4 skate wings
- 60g unsalted butter
- 2 tablespoons capers, drained
- Zest and juice of 1 lemon
- 2 tablespoons fresh parsley, chopped
- Salt and pepper to taste

Instructions
1. Preheat the Ninja Dual Zone Air Fryer to 400°F using the Grill mode.
2. Season skate wings with salt and pepper.
3. Grill skate wings for about 4-5 minutes per side or until the flesh is opaque and easily flakes.
4. In a small pan, melt unsalted butter and add capers, lemon zest, and lemon juice.
5. Cook the butter mixture until it turns golden brown.
6. Pour the black butter sauce over the grilled skate wings.
7. Sprinkle chopped fresh parsley on top.
8. Serve the Skate with Black Butter for a delectable seafood dish.

Seafood Paella

Prep time: 20 minutes Cook time: 30 minutes Serves 6

Ingredients
- 360g Arborio rice
- 500g mixed seafood (shrimp, mussels, squid)
- 1 onion, finely chopped
- 2 cloves garlic, minced
- 1 red bell pepper, diced
- 1 tomato, diced
- 1 teaspoon smoked paprika
- 1 teaspoon saffron threads, soaked in 60ml warm water
- Zest and juice of 1 lemon
- 960ml fish stock
- Salt and pepper to taste
- Fresh parsley, chopped (for garnish)

Instructions
1. Preheat the Ninja Dual Zone Air Fryer to 375°F using the Bake mode.
2. In a paella pan or oven-safe dish, sauté chopped onion and minced garlic until softened.
3. Add Arborio rice and cook until lightly toasted.
4. Stir in diced red bell pepper, diced tomato, smoked paprika, and soaked saffron threads.
5. Arrange mixed seafood on top of the rice mixture.
6. Pour fish stock over the paella and season with salt and pepper.
7. Place lemon slices on the seafood.
8. Bake for about 25-30 minutes or until the rice is tender and seafood is cooked.
9. Garnish the Seafood Paella with chopped fresh parsley before serving.

Baked Gurnard with Cherry Tomato

Prep time: 15 minutes   Cook time: 20 minutes   Serves 4

Ingredients
- 4 gurnard fillets
- 2 tablespoons olive oil
- 1 onion, finely chopped
- 2 cloves garlic, minced
- 400g cherry tomatoes, halved
- 1 teaspoon dried oregano
- Salt and pepper to taste
- Fresh parsley, chopped (for garnish)
- Lemon wedges (for serving)

Instructions
1. Preheat the Ninja Dual Zone Air Fryer to 375°F using the Bake mode.
2. Place gurnard fillets in a baking dish and drizzle with olive oil.
3. In a skillet, sauté chopped onion and minced garlic until softened.
4. Add cherry tomatoes, Kalamata olives, dried oregano, salt, and pepper to the skillet. Cook for 5 minutes.
5. Spoon the tomato and olive mixture over the gurnard fillets.
6. Bake for about 15-20 minutes or until the fish is cooked through and flakes easily.
7. Garnish with chopped fresh parsley.
8. Serve the Baked Gurnard with Cherry Tomato with lemon wedges for a delightful and flavourful dish.

Chapter 6
Sides and Appetisers

Courgette Fries

Prep time: 15 minutes Cook time: 15 minutes Serves 4

Ingredients
- 2 large courgettes (zucchinis), cut into fries
- 2 tablespoons olive oil
- 1 teaspoon garlic powder
- 1 teaspoon paprika
- Salt and pepper to taste
- 2 tablespoons grated Parmesan cheese (optional)

Instructions
1. Preheat the Ninja Dual Zone Air Fryer to 375°F using the Air Fry mode.
2. In a bowl, toss courgette fries with olive oil, garlic powder, paprika, salt, and pepper.
3. Arrange the fries in the air fryer basket, ensuring they are in a single layer.
4. Air fry for about 12-15 minutes, shaking the basket halfway through, until the fries are golden and crisp.
5. Optional: Sprinkle grated Parmesan cheese over the fries during the last 2 minutes of cooking.
6. Serve the Courgette Fries as a tasty and healthier alternative to traditional fries.

Baked Camembert with RedCurrant Jelly

Prep time: 5 minutes Cook time: 15 minutes Serves 4

Ingredients
- 1 whole Camembert cheese
- 2 tablespoons red currant jelly
- Fresh rosemary sprigs (for garnish)
- Sliced baguette or crackers (for serving)

Instructions
1. Preheat the Ninja Dual Zone Air Fryer to 375°F using the Bake mode.
2. Remove any packaging from the Camembert and place it in a small oven-safe dish.
3. Score the top of the cheese in a crisscross pattern.
4. Spoon red currant jelly over the top of the Camembert.
5. Bake for about 15 minutes or until the cheese is gooey and slightly golden.
6. Garnish with fresh rosemary sprigs.
7. Serve the Baked Camembert with Red Currant Jelly alongside sliced baguette or crackers for a delightful appetiser.

Parmesan and Garlic Roasted Brussels Sprouts

Prep time: 10 minutes   Cook time: 15 minutes   Serves 4

Ingredients
- 500g Brussels sprouts, halved
- 2 tablespoons olive oil
- 2 cloves garlic, minced
- 2 tablespoons grated Parmesan cheese
- Salt and pepper to taste
- Lemon wedges (for serving)

Instructions
1. Preheat the Ninja Dual Zone Air Fryer to 375°F using the Air Fry mode.
2. In a bowl, toss halved Brussels sprouts with olive oil, minced garlic, Parmesan cheese, salt, and pepper.
3. Arrange the Brussels sprouts in the air fryer basket, ensuring they are in a single layer.
4. Air fry for about 12-15 minutes, shaking the basket halfway through, until the Brussels sprouts are golden and crispy.
5. Squeeze fresh lemon juice over the roasted Brussels sprouts before serving.

Liver and Bacon on Crusty Bread

Prep time: 10 minutes   Cook time: 15 minutes   Serves 4

Ingredients
- 500g lamb or beef liver, sliced
- 8 slices crusty bread
- 8 rashers of bacon
- 2 onions, thinly sliced
- 2 tablespoons olive oil
- Salt and pepper to taste
- Fresh parsley, chopped (for garnish)

Instructions
1. Preheat the Ninja Dual Zone Air Fryer to 400°F using the Grill mode.
2. In a skillet, cook bacon until crispy. Remove and set aside.
3. In the same skillet, add olive oil and sauté sliced liver and onions until liver is cooked and onions are caramelised.
4. Grill the crusty bread slices until golden and crisp.
5. Assemble the liver and bacon on the crusty bread slices.
6. Season with salt and pepper, and garnish with chopped fresh parsley.
7. Serve the Liver and Bacon on Crusty Bread as a hearty and flavourful appetiser or light meal.

Scotch Woodcock (Anchovy on Toast)

Prep time: 10 minutes   Cook time: 5 minutes   Serves 4

Ingredients
- 8 slices whole-grain bread
- 1 can anchovies in oil, drained
- 4 tablespoons unsalted butter
- 4 large eggs
- Salt and pepper to taste
- Fresh chives, chopped (for garnish)

Instructions
1. Preheat the Ninja Dual Zone Air Fryer to 400°F using the Grill mode.
2. Grill the whole-grain bread slices until toasted.
3. In a bowl, mash anchovies with softened butter to create a paste.
4. Spread the anchovy butter on the toasted bread slices.
5. In a separate pan, fry eggs to your liking.
6. Place a fried egg on top of each anchovy-covered toast.
7. Season with salt and pepper, and garnish with chopped fresh chives.
8. Serve Scotch Woodcock (Anchovy on Toast) as a savory and indulgent snack.

Crispy Baked Goat Cheese Balls

Prep time: 20 minutes   Cook time: 15 minutes   Serves 4

Ingredients
- 150g goat cheese, chilled and crumbled
- 60g breadcrumbs
- 1 tablespoon fresh parsley, finely chopped
- 1 egg, beaten
- Salt and pepper to taste
- Olive oil spray

Instructions
1. Preheat the Ninja Dual Zone Air Fryer to 375°F using the Bake mode.
2. In a bowl, combine crumbled goat cheese, 60g breadcrumbs, chopped fresh parsley, beaten egg, salt, and pepper.
3. Form the mixture into small balls and place them on a baking sheet.
4. Lightly spray the goat cheese balls with olive oil.
5. Bake for about 15 minutes or until the balls are golden and crispy.
6. Allow them to cool for a few minutes before serving.
7. Serve these Crispy Baked Goat Cheese Balls as a delightful and crunchy appetiser.

Bubble and Squeak Patties

Prep time: 15 minutes   Cook time: 15 minutes   Serves 4

Ingredients
- 500g mashed potatoes, cold
- 200g Brussels sprouts, cooked and chopped
- 1 small onion, finely chopped
- 2 tablespoons butter, melted
- Salt and pepper to taste
- 1 tablespoon vegetable oil (for brushing)

Instructions
1. Preheat the Ninja Dual Zone Air Fryer to 375°F using the Air Fry mode.
2. In a bowl, mix cold mashed potatoes, chopped Brussels sprouts, finely chopped onion, melted butter, salt, and pepper.
3. Form the mixture into small patties and place them on the air fryer basket.
4. Brush the patties with vegetable oil.
5. Air fry for about 12-15 minutes, turning halfway through, until the Bubble and Squeak Patties are golden and crisp.
6. Serve and enjoy.

Bacon-Wrapped Dates with Blue Cheese

Prep time: 15 minutes   Cook time: 12 minutes   Serves 4

Ingredients
- 16 Medjool dates, pitted
- 8 slices bacon, cut in half
- 80g blue cheese, crumbled
- Fresh thyme leaves (for garnish)

Instructions
1. Preheat the Ninja Dual Zone Air Fryer to 375°F using the Air Fry mode.
2. Stuff each pitted date with crumbled blue cheese.
3. Wrap each date with half a slice of bacon, securing it with a toothpick.
4. Arrange the bacon-wrapped dates in the air fryer basket.
5. Air fry for about 10-12 minutes or until the bacon is crispy.
6. Remove toothpicks before serving.
7. Garnish with fresh thyme leaves.

Smoked Haddock Scotch Eggs with Hollandaise Sauce

Prep time: 20 minutes　　　Cook time: 15 minutes　　　Serves 4

Ingredients
- 4 large eggs
- 120g breadcrumbs
- 300g smoked haddock, cooked and flaked
- 1 tablespoon fresh parsley, chopped
- Salt and pepper to taste
- 60g all-purpose flour
- 30ml vegetable oil
- 1 batch Hollandaise sauce (see below)
- Hollandaise Sauce:
- 3 large egg yolks
- 15ml lemon juice
- 120g unsalted butter, melted
- Salt and cayenne pepper to taste

Instructions
1. In a blender, combine egg yolks and lemon juice. Blend until smooth.
2. While the blender is running, slowly pour in the melted butter until the sauce thickens.
3. Season with salt and cayenne pepper. Set aside.

Scotch Eggs Preparation Instructions:
1. Preheat the Ninja Dual Zone Air Fryer to 375°F using the Air Fry mode.
2. Place eggs in a saucepan, cover with water, and boil for 6 minutes. Peel and set aside.
3. In a bowl, mix flaked smoked haddock, breadcrumbs, chopped parsley, salt, and pepper.
4. Flatten a portion of the haddock mixture, encase a boiled egg, and shape into a ball.
5. Roll each ball in flour, ensuring even coating.
6. Air fry for about 12-15 minutes or until the Scotch eggs are golden and crispy.
7. Serve the Smoked Haddock Scotch
8. Eggs with Hollandaise Sauce for a flavourful and indulgent pre-meal experience.

Black Pudding Crostini with Pear Chutney

Prep time: 20 minutes　　　Cook time: 15 minutes　　　Serves 4

Ingredients
- 200g black pudding, sliced
- 8 slices baguette, toasted
- 1 large pear, finely chopped
- 2 tablespoons red onion, finely chopped
- 2 tablespoons apple cider vinegar
- 1 tablespoon brown sugar
- 1/2 teaspoon ground cinnamon
- Fresh parsley, chopped (for garnish)

Instructions
1. Preheat the Ninja Dual Zone Air Fryer to 375°F using the Air Fry mode.
2. Air fry the black pudding slices until crispy, about 8-10 minutes.
3. In a saucepan, combine chopped pear, red onion, apple cider vinegar, brown sugar, and ground cinnamon. Cook over medium heat until the mixture thickens, stirring occasionally.
4. Top each toasted baguette slice with a piece of crispy black pudding and a spoonful of pear chutney.
5. Garnish with chopped fresh parsley before serving.

Ploughman's Platter Bites

Prep time: 15 minutes　　Cook time: 10 minutes　　Serves 4

Ingredients
- 8 mini cheddar cheese cubes
- 8 cherry tomatoes, halved
- 4 small pickles, sliced
- 4 slices of cooked ham, cut into squares
- 1 apple, sliced
- Eggs
- Branston pickle or chutney (for dipping)

Instructions
1. Preheat the Ninja Dual Zone Air Fryer to 375°F using the Air Fry mode.
2. Arrange mini cheddar cheese cubes, halved cherry tomatoes, pickle slices, squares of cooked ham, and apple slices on the air fryer basket.
3. Air fry for about 5-7 minutes or until the cheese is slightly melted and ingredients are warmed.
4. Serve Ploughman's Platter Bites with a side of Branston pickle or chutney for dipping.
5. Enjoy these bite-sized delights inspired by the classic Ploughman's lunch.

Stilton and Pear Crostini

Prep time: 15 minutes　　Cook time: 10 minutes　　Serves 4

Ingredients
- 100g Stilton cheese, crumbled
- 1 large pear, thinly sliced
- 8 slices baguette, toasted
- Honey (for drizzling)
- Walnuts, chopped (for garnish)

Instructions
1. Preheat the Ninja Dual Zone Air Fryer to 375°F using the Air Fry mode.
2. Air fry the baguette slices until golden and crisp, about 8-10 minutes.
3. Top each toasted baguette slice with crumbled Stilton cheese and a slice of pear.
4. Drizzle honey over the Stilton and pear.
5. Garnish with chopped walnuts.

Marmite and Cheese Swirls

Prep time: 15 minutes Cook time: 12 minutes Serves 4

Ingredients
- 1 sheet puff pastry (store-bought or homemade)
- 2 tablespoons Marmite
- 120g cheddar cheese, grated
- 1 tablespoon butter, melted (for brushing)

Instructions
1. Preheat the Ninja Dual Zone Air Fryer to 375°F using the Air Fry mode.
2. Roll out the puff pastry on a floured surface into a rectangle.
3. Spread Marmite evenly over the puff pastry.
4. Sprinkle grated cheddar cheese over the Marmite layer.
5. Starting from one edge, tightly roll the pastry into a log.
6. Cut the log into slices, about 1 inch thick.
7. Place the swirls on the air fryer basket, leaving space between each.
8. Air fry for about 10-12 minutes or until the swirls are golden and puffed.
9. Brush the swirls with melted butter after removing them from the air fryer.
10. Serve hot.

Chapter 7
Vegan and Veggies

Vegan Falafel

Prep time: 15 minutes　　Cook time: 15 minutes　　Serves 4

Ingredients
- 1 can (400g) chickpeas, drained and rinsed
- 60g fresh parsley, chopped
- 30g red onion, finely chopped
- 2 cloves garlic, minced
- 1 teaspoon ground cumin
- 1 teaspoon ground coriander
- 1/2 teaspoon baking soda
- Salt and pepper to taste
- 2 tablespoons all-purpose flour
- 2 tablespoons olive oil (for brushing)

Instructions
1. In a food processor, combine chickpeas, parsley, red onion, garlic, cumin, coriander, baking soda, salt, and pepper. Pulse until the mixture is well combined but still slightly chunky.
2. Transfer the mixture to a bowl and stir in all-purpose flour. Form into small falafel patties.
3. Preheat the Ninja Dual Zone Air Fryer to 375°F using the Air Fry mode.
4. Brush falafel patties with olive oil and place them on the air fryer basket.
5. Air fry for about 12-15 minutes, turning halfway through, until the falafel are golden and crispy.
6. Serve Vegan Falafel with your favourite dipping sauce or in pita pockets with veggies.

Roasted Vegetable Kebabs

Prep time: 15 minutes　　Cook time: 20 minutes　　Serves 4

Ingredients
- 1 red bell pepper, cut into chunks
- 1 yellow bell pepper, cut into chunks
- 1 zucchini, sliced
- 1 red onion, cut into wedges
- Cherry tomatoes
- 2 tablespoons olive oil
- 1 teaspoon dried oregano
- Salt and pepper to taste
- Wooden skewers

Instructions
1. Preheat the Ninja Dual Zone Air Fryer to 375°F using the Air Fry mode.
2. In a bowl, toss bell peppers, zucchini, red onion, and cherry tomatoes with olive oil, dried oregano, salt, and pepper.
3. Thread the vegetables onto wooden skewers.
4. Place the skewers on the air fryer basket.
5. Air fry for about 18-20 minutes or until the vegetables are tender and slightly charred.

Baked Sweet Potato Fries

Prep time: 10 minutes   Cook time: 20 minutes   Serves 4

Ingredients
- 2 large sweet potatoes, cut into fries
- 1 tablespoon olive oil
- 1 teaspoon paprika
- 1/2 teaspoon garlic powder
- 1/2 teaspoon cumin
- Salt and pepper to taste

Instructions
1. Preheat the Ninja Dual Zone Air Fryer to 375°F using the Air Fry mode.
2. In a bowl, toss sweet potato fries with olive oil, paprika, garlic powder, cumin, salt, and pepper.
3. Place the fries on the air fryer basket.
4. Air fry for about 18-20 minutes, shaking the basket halfway through, until the sweet potato fries are crispy and golden.

Vegan Sausages

Prep time: 15 minutes   Cook time: 15 minutes   Serves 4

Ingredients
- 4 vegan sausages
- 1 tablespoon olive oil
- 1 teaspoon smoked paprika
- 1/2 teaspoon garlic powder
- 1/2 teaspoon onion powder
- Salt and pepper to taste

Instructions
1. Preheat the Ninja Dual Zone Air Fryer to 375°F using the Air Fry mode.
2. In a bowl, mix olive oil, smoked paprika, garlic powder, onion powder, salt, and pepper.
3. Coat vegan sausages with the spice mixture.
4. Place the sausages on the air fryer basket.
5. Air fry for about 12-15 minutes, turning halfway through, until the sausages are browned and cooked through.

Stuffed Mushrooms

Prep time: 15 minutes Cook time: 15 minutes Serves 4

Ingredients
- 8 large mushrooms, cleaned and stems removed
- 120ml breadcrumbs
- 60ml vegan cream cheese
- 2 tablespoons fresh parsley, chopped
- 1 clove garlic, minced
- Salt and pepper to taste
- Olive oil spray

Instructions
1. Preheat the Ninja Dual Zone Air Fryer to 375°F using the Air Fry mode.
2. In a bowl, mix breadcrumbs, vegan cream cheese, parsley, garlic, salt, and pepper.
3. Stuff each mushroom cap with the breadcrumb mixture.
4. Place the stuffed mushrooms on the air fryer basket.
5. Lightly spray with olive oil.
6. Air fry for about 12-15 minutes, until the mushrooms are tender and the tops are golden.

Roasted Brussels Sprouts

Prep time: 10 minutes Cook time: 15 minutes Serves 4

Ingredients
- 500g Brussels sprouts, trimmed and halved
- 2 tablespoons olive oil
- 1 teaspoon garlic powder
- 1/2 teaspoon smoked paprika
- Salt and pepper to taste

Instructions
1. Preheat the Ninja Dual Zone Air Fryer to 375°F using the Air Fry mode.
2. In a bowl, toss Brussels sprouts with olive oil, garlic powder, smoked paprika, salt, and pepper.
3. Place the Brussels sprouts on the air fryer basket.
4. Air fry for about 12-15 minutes, shaking the basket halfway through, until the Brussels sprouts are crispy and golden.

Baked Butternut Squash Risotto

Prep time: 15 minutes　　Cook time: 40 minutes　　Serves 4

Ingredients
- 200g Arborio rice
- 1/2 butternut squash, peeled and diced
- 1 onion, finely chopped
- 2 cloves garlic, minced
- 950ml vegetable broth
- 120ml white wine
- 30ml olive oil
- 120ml nutritional yeast
- Salt and pepper to taste
- Fresh parsley for garnish

Instructions
1. Preheat the Ninja Dual Zone Air Fryer to 375°F using the Bake mode.
2. In a baking dish, combine Arborio rice, butternut squash, onion, garlic, vegetable broth, white wine, olive oil, and nutritional yeast.
3. Season with salt and pepper to taste. Mix well.
4. Bake for about 40 minutes or until the rice is cooked, and the butternut squash is tender.
5. Garnish with fresh parsley before serving.

Fried Tofu Stir-fry

Prep time: 15 minutes　　Cook time: 15 minutes　　Serves 4

Ingredients
- 400g firm tofu, pressed and cubed
- 240g mixed vegetables (broccoli, bell peppers, snap peas)
- 45ml soy sauce
- 15ml hoisin sauce
- 15ml sesame oil
- 5g cornstarch
- 5g ginger, minced
- 1 clove garlic, minced
- 30ml vegetable oil
- Green onions for garnish

Instructions
1. Preheat the Ninja Dual Zone Air Fryer to 375°F using the Air Fry mode.
2. In a bowl, combine soy sauce, hoisin sauce, sesame oil, cornstarch, ginger, and garlic.
3. Toss tofu cubes in the sauce mixture until well coated.
4. Air fry tofu for about 15 minutes, turning halfway through, until golden and crispy.
5. In a stir-fry pan, heat vegetable oil, add mixed vegetables, and stir-fry until tender.
6. Add air-fried tofu to the vegetables, toss together, and garnish with green onions.

Vegan Spring Rolls

Prep time: 20 minutes   Cook time: 10 minutes   Serves 4

Ingredients
- 8 spring roll wrappers
- 240g shredded cabbage
- 240ml soy sauce
- 120ml rice vinegar
- 1 tablespoon maple syrup
- 1 teaspoon sesame oil
- 1 teaspoon grated ginger
- 1 clove garlic, minced
- 1 carrot, julienned
- 1 cucumber, julienned
- Fresh cilantro leaves

Instructions
1. Preheat the Ninja Dual Zone Air Fryer to 375°F using the Air Fry mode.
2. In a bowl, whisk together soy sauce, rice vinegar, maple syrup, sesame oil, grated ginger, and minced garlic to make the dipping sauce.
3. Lay out a spring roll wrapper, place shredded cabbage, carrot, cucumber, and cilantro leaves in the center.
4. Roll up the spring roll, folding in the sides, and seal the edge with a bit of water.
5. Place the spring rolls on the air fryer basket.
6. Air fry for about 8-10 minutes, turning halfway through, until they are golden and crispy.
7. Serve with the prepared dipping sauce.

Roasted Cauliflower Steaks

Prep time: 10 minutes   Cook time: 25 minutes   Serves 4

Ingredients
- 1 large cauliflower head, sliced into steaks
- 30ml olive oil
- 1 teaspoon smoked paprika
- 1 teaspoon garlic powder
- Salt and pepper to taste
- Fresh parsley for garnish

Instructions
1. Preheat the Ninja Dual Zone Air Fryer to 400°F using the Roast mode.
2. In a bowl, mix olive oil, smoked paprika, garlic powder, salt, and pepper.
3. Brush both sides of cauliflower steaks with the oil mixture.
4. Place cauliflower steaks on the air fryer basket.
5. Roast for about 25 minutes or until golden brown, flipping halfway through.
6. Garnish with fresh parsley before serving.

Baked Aubergine Parmesan

Prep time: 15 minutes | Cook time: 30 minutes | Serves 4

Ingredients
- 2 large aubergines, sliced
- 120g breadcrumbs
- 240ml marinara sauce
- 120g vegan mozzarella cheese, shredded
- 60g vegan Parmesan cheese, grated
- Fresh basil for garnish

Instructions
1. Preheat the Ninja Dual Zone Air Fryer to 375°F using the Bake mode.
2. Coat aubergine slices in breadcrumbs and arrange them on the air fryer basket.
3. Bake for about 15 minutes, flipping halfway through.
4. In a baking dish, layer marinara sauce, baked aubergine slices, and cheeses.
5. Repeat the layers, finishing with a layer of cheese on top.
6. Bake for an additional 15 minutes or until the cheese is melted and bubbly.
7. Garnish with fresh basil before serving.

Fried Plantain Slices

Prep time: 10 minutes | Cook time: 15 minutes | Serves 4

Ingredients
- 2 ripe plantains, peeled and sliced
- 30ml vegetable oil
- 1 teaspoon cinnamon
- 1/4 teaspoon salt

Instructions
1. Preheat the Ninja Dual Zone Air Fryer to 375°F using the Air Fry mode.
2. In a bowl, toss plantain slices with vegetable oil, cinnamon, and salt.
3. Place plantain slices on the air fryer basket.
4. Air fry for about 15 minutes, shaking the basket halfway through, until golden brown.
5. Serve these delicious fried plantain slices as a tasty snack or side dish.

Vegan Chickpea Patties

Prep time: 15 minutes Cook time: 20 minutes Serves 4

Ingredients
- 1 can (400g) chickpeas, drained and rinsed
- 60g breadcrumbs
- 30g chopped onion
- 2 cloves garlic, minced
- 1 teaspoon ground cumin
- 1 teaspoon paprika
- Salt and pepper to taste
- 30ml olive oil (for brushing)

Instructions
1. In a food processor, combine chickpeas, breadcrumbs, chopped onion, minced garlic, ground cumin, paprika, salt, and pepper.
2. Pulse until the mixture is well combined but still has some texture.
3. Shape the mixture into patties and place them on the air fryer basket.
4. Brush each patty with olive oil.
5. Air fry at 375°F for about 20 minutes, turning halfway through, until the patties are golden and crisp.
6. Serve the vegan chickpea patties with your favourite dipping sauce.

Vegan Potato Rosti

Prep time: 15 minutes Cook time: 25 minutes Serves 4

Ingredients
- 4 medium potatoes, peeled and grated
- 30g finely chopped onion
- 2 tablespoons flour
- Salt and pepper to taste
- 30ml olive oil (for brushing)

Instructions
1. In a bowl, combine grated potatoes, chopped onion, flour, salt, and pepper.
2. Shape the mixture into rosti patties and place them on the air fryer basket.
3. Brush each rosti with olive oil.
4. Air fry at 375°F for about 25 minutes, turning halfway through, until the rosti are golden and crispy.
5. Serve the vegan potato rosti as a delicious side dish.

Roasted Tomato and Chickpea Salad

Prep time: 10 minutes | Cook time: 20 minutes | Serves 4

Ingredients
- 300g cherry tomatoes, halved
- 1 can (400g) chickpeas, drained and rinsed
- 2 tablespoons olive oil
- 1 teaspoon dried oregano
- Salt and pepper to taste
- Fresh basil leaves for garnish

Instructions
1. Preheat the Ninja Dual Zone Air Fryer to 400°F using the Roast mode.
2. In a bowl, toss cherry tomatoes and chickpeas with olive oil, dried oregano, salt, and pepper.
3. Spread the mixture on the air fryer basket.
4. Roast for about 20 minutes or until the tomatoes are blistered and the chickpeas are golden.
5. Garnish with fresh basil leaves before serving.

Chapter 8
Sweet Snacks and Desserts

Chocolate and Beetroot Cake

Prep time: 20 minutes   Cook time: 40 minutes   Serves 8

Ingredients
- 200g cooked beetroots, pureed
- 200g dark chocolate, melted
- 150g unsalted butter, softened
- 200g granulated sugar
- 3 large eggs
- 200g all-purpose flour
- 1 teaspoon baking powder
- 1/2 teaspoon baking soda
- 50g cocoa powder
- 120ml buttermilk
- 1 teaspoon vanilla extract
- Powdered sugar (for dusting)

Instructions
1. Preheat the Ninja Dual Zone Air Fryer to 350°F using the Bake mode.
2. In a bowl, mix together pureed beetroots, melted dark chocolate, softened butter, and granulated sugar.
3. Add eggs one at a time, beating well after each addition.
4. In a separate bowl, sift together all-purpose flour, baking powder, baking soda, and cocoa powder.
5. Gradually add the dry ingredients to the wet ingredients, alternating with buttermilk.
6. Stir in vanilla extract.
7. Pour the batter into a greased cake tin.
8. Bake for about 35-40 minutes or until a toothpick inserted into the centre comes out clean.
9. Let the cake cool, then dust with powdered sugar before serving.

Raspberry Meringue Roulade

Prep time: 30 minutes   Cook time: 20 minutes   Serves 6

Ingredients
- 4 large egg whites
- 200g granulated sugar
- 1 teaspoon white vinegar
- 1 teaspoon cornstarch
- 150g fresh raspberries
- 250ml whipped cream

Instructions
1. Preheat the Ninja Dual Zone Air Fryer to 350°F using the Bake mode.
2. In a clean, dry bowl, whisk egg whites until stiff peaks form.
3. Gradually add granulated sugar, white vinegar, and cornstarch. Continue to whisk until glossy.
4. Spread the meringue mixture onto a parchment-lined baking sheet.
5. Bake for about 15-20 minutes or until the meringue is crisp on the outside.
6. Invert the baked meringue onto a clean kitchen towel.
7. Remove the parchment paper and let it cool.
8. Spread whipped cream over the meringue and scatter fresh raspberries.
9. Carefully roll the meringue into a log shape.
10. Chill before slicing and serving this delightful Raspberry Meringue Roulade.

Cherry and Almond Frangipane

Prep time: 20 minutes Cook time: 40 minutes Serves 8

Ingredients
- 1 sheet puff pastry, thawed
- 150g almond meal
- 100g granulated sugar
- 100g unsalted butter, softened
- 2 large eggs
- 1 teaspoon almond extract
- 1/2 teaspoon vanilla extract
- 150g fresh cherries, pitted and halved
- 30g flaked almonds
- Powdered sugar (for dusting)

Instructions
1. Preheat the Ninja Dual Zone Air Fryer to 375°F using the Bake mode.
2. Roll out the puff pastry and line a tart tin.
3. In a bowl, cream together almond meal, granulated sugar, softened butter, eggs, almond extract, and vanilla extract.
4. Spread the almond mixture over the puff pastry.
5. Arrange fresh cherry halves on top and sprinkle with flaked almonds.
6. Bake for about 35-40 minutes or until the frangipane is set and golden.
7. Dust with powdered sugar before serving.
8. Enjoy the delightful combination of Cherry and Almond Frangipane.

Rhubarb and Ginger Crumble

Prep time: 15 minutes Cook time: 30 minutes Serves 6

Ingredients
- 500g rhubarb, chopped
- 100g granulated sugar
- 1 tablespoon crystallized ginger, chopped
- 1 teaspoon ground ginger
- 150g all-purpose flour
- 75g rolled oats
- 75g unsalted butter, chilled and cubed
- Vanilla ice cream (for serving)

Instructions
1. Preheat the Ninja Dual Zone Air Fryer to 375°F using the Bake mode.
2. In a bowl, toss chopped rhubarb with granulated sugar and crystallized ginger.
3. Transfer the rhubarb mixture to a baking dish.
4. In another bowl, combine all-purpose flour, rolled oats, and chilled cubed butter to make the crumble topping.
5. Sprinkle the crumble topping over the rhubarb mixture.
6. Bake for about 25-30 minutes or until the crumble is golden and the rhubarb is bubbling.
7. Serve the Rhubarb and Ginger Crumble warm, and top with vanilla ice cream if desired.

Sticky Ginger Parkin

Prep time: 20 minutes | Cook time: 40 minutes | Serves 8

Ingredients
- 200g oatmeal
- 200g self-raising flour
- 1 teaspoon ground ginger
- 1/2 teaspoon ground cinnamon
- 150g unsalted butter
- 150g golden syrup
- 150g black treacle
- 150g dark brown sugar
- 2 large eggs, beaten
- 150ml milk

Instructions
1. Preheat the Ninja Dual Zone Air Fryer to 350°F using the Bake mode.
2. In a large bowl, mix oatmeal, self-raising flour, ground ginger, and ground cinnamon.
3. In a saucepan, melt unsalted butter, golden syrup, black treacle, and dark brown sugar. Let it cool slightly.
4. Pour the melted mixture into the dry ingredients, stirring well.
5. Add beaten eggs and milk to the mixture, combining thoroughly.
6. Transfer the batter to a greased baking tin.
7. Bake for about 35-40 minutes or until a skewer inserted into the center comes out clean.
8. Allow the Sticky Ginger Parkin to cool before slicing and serving.

Orange Marmalade Bread Pudding

Prep time: 15 minutes | Cook time: 30 minutes | Serves 6

Ingredients
- 6 slices of white bread, crusts removed and cut into cubes
- 3 tablespoons orange marmalade
- 2 large eggs
- 300ml milk
- 50g granulated sugar
- 1 teaspoon vanilla extract
- Zest of 1 orange
- Butter (for greasing)

Instructions
1. Preheat the Ninja Dual Zone Air Fryer to 350°F using the Bake mode.
2. Grease a baking dish with butter.
3. Place the bread cubes in the baking dish.
4. In a bowl, mix orange marmalade, eggs, milk, granulated sugar, vanilla extract, and orange zest.
5. Pour the mixture over the bread cubes, ensuring they are well-coated.
6. Let it sit for a few minutes to allow the bread to absorb the liquid.
7. Bake for about 25-30 minutes or until the pudding is set and golden.
8. Serve your delicious Orange Marmalade Bread Pudding warm and enjoy the citrus-infused goodness.

Coffee and Walnut Swiss Roll

Prep time: 20 minutes Cook time: 15 minutes Serves 8

Ingredients
- 4 large eggs
- 100g granulated sugar
- 100g self-raising flour
- 2 tablespoons instant coffee, dissolved in 2 tablespoons hot water
- 50g walnuts, chopped
- 150ml double cream
- 2 tablespoons powdered sugar (for dusting)

Instructions
1. Preheat the Ninja Dual Zone Air Fryer to 375°F using the Bake mode.
2. In a bowl, whisk eggs and granulated sugar until light and fluffy.
3. Gently fold in self-raising flour until well combined.
4. Add the dissolved instant coffee and chopped walnuts, folding into the batter.
5. Pour the batter into a lined baking tray.
6. Bake for about 12-15 minutes or until the sponge is springy to the touch.
7. While the sponge is still warm, turn it out onto a sheet of parchment paper.
8. Whip the double cream until it forms soft peaks.
9. Spread the whipped cream over the sponge, then carefully roll it up.
10. Dust with powdered sugar before serving the delightful Coffee and Walnut Swiss Roll.

Sticky Fig Parkin

Prep time: 20 minutes Cook time: 40 minutes Serves 8

Ingredients
- 200g self-raising flour
- 150g oatmeal
- 1 teaspoon ground ginger
- 150g unsalted butter
- 150g golden syrup
- 150g black treacle
- 150g dark brown sugar
- 200g dried figs, chopped
- 2 large eggs, beaten

Instructions
1. Preheat the Ninja Dual Zone Air Fryer to 350°F using the Bake mode.
2. In a large bowl, mix self-raising flour, oatmeal, and ground ginger.
3. In a saucepan, melt unsalted butter, golden syrup, black treacle, and dark brown sugar. Allow it to cool slightly.
4. Pour the melted mixture into the dry ingredients, stirring well.
5. Add beaten eggs and chopped dried figs, combining thoroughly.
6. Transfer the batter to a greased baking tin.
7. Bake for about 35-40 minutes or until a skewer inserted into the centre comes out clean.
8. Allow the Sticky Fig Parkin to cool before slicing and serving.

The Dirty Dozen and Clean Fifteen

The Environmental Working Group (EWG) is a nonprofit, nonpartisan organization dedicated to protecting human health and the environment Its mission is to empower people to live healthier lives in a healthier environment. This organization publishes an annual list of the twelve kinds of produce, in sequence, that have the highest amount of pesticide residue-the Dirty Dozen-as well as a list of the fifteen kinds ofproduce that have the least amount of pesticide residue-the Clean Fifteen.

THE DIRTY DOZEN

- The 2016 Dirty Dozen includes the following produce. These are considered among the year's most important produce to buy organic:

  - Strawberries
  - Apples
  - Nectarines
  - Peaches
  - Celery
  - Grapes
  - Cherries
  - Spinach
  - Tomatoes
  - Bell peppers
  - Cherry tomatoes
  - Cucumbers
  - Kale/collard greens
  - Hot peppers

- *The Dirty Dozen list contains two additional itemskale/collard greens and hot peppers-because they tend to contain trace levels of highly hazardous pesticides.*

THE CLEAN FIFTEEN

- The least critical to buy organically are the Clean Fifteen list. The following are on the 2016 list:

  - Avocados
  - Corn
  - Pineapples
  - Cabbage
  - Sweet peas
  - Onions
  - Asparagus
  - Mangos
  - Papayas
  - Kiw
  - Eggplant
  - Honeydew
  - Grapefruit
  - Cantaloupe
  - Cauliflower

- *Some of the sweet corn sold in the United States are made from genetically engineered (GE) seedstock. Buy organic varieties of these crops to avoid GE produce.*

MEASUREMENT CONVERSION CHART

VOLUME EQUIVALENTS(DRY)

US STANDARD	METRIC (APPROXIMATE)
1/8 teaspoon	0.5 mL
1/4 teaspoon	1 mL
1/2 teaspoon	2 mL
3/4 teaspoon	4 mL
1 teaspoon	5 mL
1 tablespoon	15 mL
1/4 cup	59 mL
1/2 cup	118 mL
3/4 cup	177 mL
1 cup	235 mL
2 cups	475 mL
3 cups	700 mL
4 cups	1 L

WEIGHT EQUIVALENTS

US STANDARD	METRIC (APPROXIMATE)
1 ounce	28 g
2 ounces	57 g
5 ounces	142 g
10 ounces	284 g
15 ounces	425 g
16 ounces (1 pound)	455 g
1.5 pounds	680 g
2 pounds	907 g

VOLUME EQUIVALENTS(LIQUID)

US STANDARD	US STANDARD (OUNCES)	METRIC (APPROXIMATE)
2 tablespoons	1 fl.oz.	30 mL
1/4 cup	2 fl.oz.	60 mL
1/2 cup	4 fl.oz.	120 mL
1 cup	8 fl.oz.	240 mL
1 1/2 cup	12 fl.oz.	355 mL
2 cups or 1 pint	16 fl.oz.	475 mL
4 cups or 1 quart	32 fl.oz.	1 L
1 gallon	128 fl.oz.	4 L

TEMPERATURES EQUIVALENTS

FAHRENHEIT(F)	CELSIUS(C) (APPROXIMATE)
225 °F	107 °C
250 °F	120 °C
275 °F	135 °C
300 °F	150 °C
325 °F	160 °C
350 °F	180 °C
375 °F	190 °C
400 °F	205 °C
425 °F	220 °C
450 °F	235 °C
475 °F	245 °C
500 °F	260 °C

Printed in Great Britain
by Amazon